PAT

Patricia FitzPatri
ogist with the Hea … om
2005 to 2017 and … xperience of
working within the I … rvice.

Specialising in parenting skills, Patricia continues to work with parents to support the social, emotional and academic development of children. Patricia's approach is influenced by parenting programmes such as Systematic Training for Effective Parenting (STEP), Incredible Years and EarlyBird, which she has used throughout her career. The contents of this book are based on Patricia's own experience as a parent and on her experience of working with parents, facilitating parenting programmes and supporting parents, carers and other professionals who work to support families.

Since retiring from the HSE in January 2017, Patricia has continued to work with parents in private practice. She also enjoys contributing to the media on topics of interest to parents and families. When not working or writing this book, she enjoys spending time with her family and friends (and rather too much time convincing her husband, John, to join her for another holiday on the byroads of rural France).

Effective Parenting

Patricia FitzPatrick

First published in 2018 by
Patricia FitzPatrick
pafitzp@gmail.com

Cover illustration by Karoline Scorzato FitzPatrick
with input from Dee FitzPatrick

Produced by:
Kells Publishing Company Ltd
Kells Publishing Company is not the publisher of this work. All rights and responsibilities remain with the author.

ISBN 978-1-9993209-0-4

Dedication

This book is dedicated to all the parents I have worked with and continue to work with. My admiration for you is limitless. My gratitude for sharing a small part of your journey is immense.

Acknowledgements

This book would not have been written had Dr Paula Cummins, a wonderful former colleague, not suggested it. I owe Paula a huge debt of gratitude for her encouragement and support at every step of the way. She has devoted many hours to reading drafts and to making suggestions.

I also want to acknowledge the support and encouragement of my children, Joe, Emer, Deirdre and Eoin, and my perpetually tolerant husband, John. My own adventures in parenting inspired me not only to learn more and seek greater understanding but also to share that knowledge with others.

Lastly, I would like to acknowledge and humbly thank Kennas Fitzsimons of Kells Publishing Company for his advice, support and tremendous work to ensure Paula's suggestion became a book.

Contents

Introduction

Parents should not be judged as *good* or *bad*. The vast majority of parents are 'good'. A good parent does three things:

- Feeds the child;
- Clothes the child;
- Provides shelter for the child.

A tiny minority of parents are either unable or too absorbed in their own wants and desires to do some or all of the above. However, what all parents need to strive towards is being EFFECTIVE.

The effective parent

An EFFECTIVE PARENT creates a home which facilitates the child's development into an emotionally secure, kind, compassionate, generous, caring and tolerant adult. You will achieve 'effective parenting' if you:

1. Focus daily on building and sustaining a POSITIVE RELATIONSHIP with your child;

2. Educate yourself on your role in supporting your child's EMOTIONAL, SOCIAL and ACADEMIC DEVELOPMENT. Then develop and use the appropriate skills in your daily interactions with your child;
3. Ensure your child's safety by having and enforcing appropriate RULES and BOUNDARIES;
4. Facilitate the development of good PROBLEM-SOLVING SKILLS in your child.

What to expect from this book

Part 1 of this book aims to provide you, the parent, with EFFECTIVE PARENTING SKILLS.

Building and maintaining a POSITIVE RELATIONSHIP with your child is central to being an EFFECTIVE PARENT, and is the topic of Chapter 1.

Chapter 2 focuses on the essential but often overlooked importance of developing your child's EMOTIONAL VOCABULARY and EMOTIONAL INTELLIGENCE.

Developing your child's SOCIAL SKILLS, and thus supporting your child to be a friendly, kind, tolerant, generous and polite individual, is discussed in Chapter 3.

Chapter 4 focuses on the ACADEMIC DEVELOPMENT of your child. The world around your child is a fascinating place, with learning opportunities everywhere. With your informed support, your child can achieve all that is uniquely possible to him.

Rules and limits are discussed in Chapter 5. This chapter also attempts to shed light on the fundamental and important difference between DISCIPLINE and PUNISHMENT.

Chapter 6 incorporates a number of the topics and skills discussed in the previous chapters in order to provide you with the necessary skills to support your child in developing EFFECTIVE PROBLEM-SOLVING SKILLS.

Part 2 brings all the skills together to find EFFECTIVE SOLUTIONS for common and not so common MISBEHAVIOURS such as:

- Biting;
- Children fighting;
- Refusing to do as told.

And PROBLEMS such as:

- Bullying;
- Anxiety;
- Food and mealtime issues;
- Tantrums and meltdowns.

The first chapter of Part 2 explores the essential topic of ATTENTION. A comprehensive understanding of the importance of increasing positive attention and decreasing negative attention is fundamental to the practice of EFFECTIVE PARENTING.

Part 1

1

Building a positive relationship

Having a positive relationship with your child is the foundation stone on which all other aspects of EFFECTIVE PARENTING are dependent. A positive relationship is one of mutual satisfaction and good feelings.

Take a few minutes and think of the people whose company you enjoy...

Now concentrate on one of those people, perhaps the one you consider your best friend, and ask yourself the following questions:

- What is it about my relationship with this person that makes it special?
- What are the key elements of this relationship?

In my experience, when parents are asked these questions the answers are generally the same and include:

- Having fun with;
- Being listened to;
- No harsh criticisms;
- Honesty – if she tells me it, I can believe it;

- Loyalty – he will stick by me, even if I make a fool of myself.

If the fun leaves the relationship, if you no longer feel listened to, if you cannot believe what this person says, if you can no longer rely on this person to be on your side, even when you make mistakes, *the relationship is in deep trouble.*

Positive relationships share the same qualities whether they are adult-to-adult relationships or parent-to-child relationships.

The fundamental difference is that:

> ADULT RELATIONSHIPS ARE A TWO-WAY STREET AND MUST BE WORKED ON BY BOTH PARTIES.

However:

> THE QUALITY OF THE RELATIONSHIP WITH YOUR CHILD IS TOTALLY DEPENDENT ON YOU. IT IS YOU AND ONLY YOU WHO CAN BUILD A POSITIVE RELATIONSHIP WITH YOUR CHILD. TEMPERAMENT TYPE (discussed further in Chapter 2) CAN MAKE THE PROCESS EASIER OR HARDER.

The aim of this first chapter is to introduce you, the parent, to the key elements involved in building and maintaining a positive relationship with your child. These elements are:

- Facial expressions that communicate love;
- Ten to twenty minutes play/special time with your child a day;

- Lots of praise and encouragement for your child's efforts and achievements;
- The appropriate use of rewards to encourage desired behaviours.

Building a positive relationship

The key principle involved in building a positive relationship with your child is to give your child lots of POSITIVE ATTENTION. You do this in a number of ways.

1. Good faces... smile, smile, smile...

Become aware of the face you present to your child. Often, a parent/caregiver is preoccupied with other important matters and her face displays stress, worry, anger, sadness, etc.

Children are acutely attuned to the face of their caregiver and to adult faces in general. Small children are also egocentric (the world revolves around them – they make things happen, they believe) and so they interpret this look on the adult's face as being caused by them and they become afraid.

Depending on the child's particular circumstances, temperament, needs, age, stage, etc, he does something to alleviate his own fear. For instance, some children may act silly in an effort to make the parent/caregiver laugh. Depending on what is going on for the parent at that time, the parent may respond with irritation and now the child feels more afraid. Confusion and anger may also enter the mix of emotions. This ups the ante for the child and he reacts to the parent's negative response to him with a negative response of his own, and the situation escalates. Nobody is feeling good here...

This can be avoided by the parent/caregiver becoming aware of the message the child is receiving from his/her face at all times. Think of how you feel when the person serving you in a shop smiles and is polite to you. That person has lots going on in her life but she puts it behind her for the moments of her interaction with you. Perhaps you are that person, serving the public. Think of how you respond to customers, clients, friends, colleagues, neighbours and others when you meet them.

> So, SHOW YOUR CHILD A PLEASANT FACE. MAKE A COMMITMENT TO SMILING AT YOUR CHILD AS OFTEN AS POSSIBLE WHEN YOU ARE IN HER COMPANY

2. PLAY

Play is a child's work. Children learn from play.[1] Although there may be disagreement on what the child learns, there is agreement that play is vital to the healthy development of the child.[2] Adults sometimes make the mistake of believing that time spent playing with their child is of little value. On the contrary, it is of immense value. In my experience, whenever a parent seeks help for behavioural problems with their child, there is little, if any, play time between parent and child. It is also my experience that when the parent introduces play time, as outlined below, the behavioural problems subside. It is also worthy of note that while young children engage in a certain amount of spontaneous play, adult intervention is necessary if the child's play is to develop creatively.[3] Therefore, playing with your child from infancy is the key element of EFFECTIVE PARENTING.

Older children (aged between 8 and 12) and teenagers may consider the term 'play' a little babyish. If this is the case, consider using an alternative such as special time/fun time/our time, or any term that your child is happy with and identifies a small block of time when you are fully present in a fun way with your child. Older children and teenagers still need your undivided attention for a short time each day, in order to facilitate a continuing positive relationship with you. The teenager's interests will have matured or changed and your role is to adapt the special time to this. For instance, a pre-teenage or teenage girl might like to experiment with her increasing interest in make-up by using you as a model. A teenage boy might like you to watch his favourite sporting activity on TV (of course, your daughter might also enjoy this). As long as the time you spend is enjoyed by your child or teenager, and for 10 to 20 minutes you are giving freely of yourself to your child, this is positive relationship building gold dust.

> AS LITTLE AS 10 MINUTES PLAYING/SPENDING SPECIAL TIME WITH YOUR CHILD EACH DAY MAKES A HUGE POSITIVE DIFFERENCE IN THE EMOTIONAL, PHYSICAL, COGNITIVE AND SPIRITUAL DEVELOPMENTAL OF YOUR CHILD.

Here are some important tips:

- LET THE CHILD CHOOSE THE ACTIVITY. Good play tools include empty boxes, building blocks, bricks, sand, paint, and arts and crafts material. Cooking and baking with your child can also be a great play activity;

- LET THE CHILD DIRECT THE PLAY. During play time, the child is in charge. Your role is to observe and comment positively on what the child is doing. Say things like: "You are putting the red brick on the black one, that's a great idea"; "Wow! What great ideas you have, that looks so comfy"; etc. Small children might like that you comment a lot. This is a fabulous opportunity for the child to learn language, meaning, shapes, colours, feelings, cause and effect, etc. Older children and teenagers may prefer less commenting, but they will know by your body language and attention that you are fully committed to making this time special;
- For this short period of time you belong completely to the child. This means giving 100% ATTENTION to the child. The phone must be turned off or left somewhere else, all screens are off – unless your play activity involves a screen;
- TRY TO PLAY EVERY DAY. The more play times a week you fit into your busy schedule, the better. For toddlers and younger children, playing a few times a day for five-to-10-minute blocks would be wonderful. But the most important thing is that you commit to playing at least once a day;
- Decide beforehand how much time you have free to spend on play. Between 10 and 20 minutes is a good recommendation for a block of play – it is difficult to sustain 100% attention for longer. Give a warning before ending your play time with the child. A five-minute

warning would sound like this: "In five more minutes, I will have to continue cooking dinner." When the five minutes are up, it is vitally important that you do not give in to the child's protest for extra time. Always think of what message your child is getting from your response.

Example

Dad is playing with his five-year-old son, Tom.

Dad: "Our play time for today is up now, Tom. I have to continue cooking dinner."

Tom: "Just another minute, *pleeease*..."

Dad: "I know you enjoyed our play time, Tom. We will do it again tomorrow. You can continue playing or you can help me by setting the table..."

It is essential that you end the play time despite the protest, as your child is always learning from your responses. Now he is learning 'trust' – do you mean what you say? He is also learning about boundaries and your ability to firmly and fairly keep the boundary. Boundaries make your child feel secure (more about this in Chapter 5). These are part of the building blocks of a positive relationship.

Parents report very little resistance to ending play when the child is offered a choice of continuing to play alone or to help the parent with a work activity, and also when the child knows that play will happen again tomorrow. Ensure that any activity is age-appropriate and safe and that your child is properly supervised. Parents also report that the child often chooses to help the parent rather than continue play. This is because it affords the child the opportunity to continue in the parent's company. However, it is very important to remember that now the parent is in charge and the child no longer has his/her full attention. This is where the concept of a 'loose neck' is important. This means that you do not ignore your child while he is quietly playing or helping you. You look around and comment, i.e. "You remembered to put the knives and forks on the table, well done!" These few words and this positive attention to your child's helpful behaviour is GOLD DUST IN TERMS OF POSITIVE RELATIONSHIP BUILDING.

For hard-to-engage children, who are not used to getting your attention in this way, playing a screen game or watching a TV programme with the child could be a great way to get started. However, as you establish a routine of regular play/special time you can suggest activities that do not involve screens.

If your child refuses your offer of play it is of great importance that you sit down and choose an activity to play with. Choose something that you think your child will be interested in and play with it yourself. The chances are very high that your child will join you. In this case, the child may be testing your commitment to her. By being available (not just saying you are available but actually showing your availability), your child knows you are serious about the importance of spending fun time with her. If your child does not join you on Day 1, don't give up. Day 2 or Day 3 may be the day your child accepts your offer. YOUR CHILD WILL ACCEPT THE OFFER SOONER RATHER THAN LATER.

Do not force your child to play. Your child may prefer to play with her friends when the weather is nice and she is allowed outdoors. Offer a time for play or special time that is likely to suit the child's routine and yours.

It is vitally important that you do not take it as a personal slight if your child refuses to engage in play or special time with you. To do so gives your child the message that *your* feelings are more important than his. It places an erroneous burden on your child to 'keep Mum or Dad happy at all costs'. This is damaging to the relationship and to your child's self-esteem.

The example below illustrates how to show your child that you are serious about re-building your relationship while at the same time respecting the child's need for autonomy.

> Aisha is aged 12 and the relationship with her mother has been strained for some time. Her mother reports Aisha as being very disrespectful and non-compliant.
>
> Aisha's mother knows that her daughter will be very suspicious of any change in behaviour on her part. Aisha is used to her mother giving out to and about her. However, she has sought advice and is committed to building the relationship with her daughter from now on, whatever it takes.

> Aisha's favourite TV programme is about to start and her mother sits down beside her on the couch.
>
> Aisha: "What are you doing here?"
>
> Mother: "I'd like to watch this programme with you."
>
> Aisha: "You hate this programme. Go away!"
>
> Mother: "I used to hate it, but you like it and I would like to give it another chance."
>
> Aisha: "You will still hate it and I won't be able to watch it... Go away!"
>
> Mother: "I would really like to watch it and I promise to stay silent..."

Aisha's body language shows hostility towards her mother, however she now starts to watch her programme. Her mother sits very quietly as close to Aisha as she knows Aisha will be comfortable with. Because of the difficulties in their relationship, it will take a few days before Aisha is comfortable with her mother sitting beside her.

If Aisha speaks to her mother during the programme or about the programme it is important to respond but not in any way that criticises the programme or Aisha's choice (if it is a programme that mother, on watching it, becomes concerned about its suitability for a 12-year-old girl, now is not the time to address that. Aisha was allowed to watch the programme before her mother sat with her. It is wonderful that now she is getting to know the programme content and that can be addressed when the relationship between mother and daughter has improved sufficiently).

Parents also report being pleasantly surprised by the confidences that children share with them during the play/special time. THE VALUE OF THIS IS IMMENSE AND IS ANOTHER EXAMPLE OF WHAT CAN BE TERMED THE GOLD DUST OF A POSITIVE RELATIONSHIP.

3. Praise

Praise is positive attention. Praise gives your child a clear message that the behaviour being praised is a valued behaviour. Parents are aware of the importance of praising their child, but often ask if you can overpraise a child. The answer is *NO*, as long as you clearly identify the behaviour you are praising – be specific, as in the examples below:

> Maria, aged 6, has just finished her dinner – eaten as much as she is hungry for. NEVER force your child to eat all on the plate.
>
> Mother: "Maria, please put your plate in the dishwasher."
>
> Marie does as she is asked.
>
> Mother: "Thanks for that Maria and also for doing it as soon as I asked. High five!"

MARIA HAS GOT THE POSITIVE ATTENTION OF PRAISE FOR COMPLIANCE AND ALSO FOR DOING IT AS SOON AS SHE WAS ASKED. SHE IS HIGHLY LIKELY TO REPEAT THIS BEHAVIOUR BECAUSE SHE LOVES PRAISE AND WANTS TO GET MORE OF IT.

Aaron, aged seven, is playing with his five-year-old brother Dan and they are having fun.

Dad: "It's lovely to see you two playing nicely together. You are great brothers to each other."

AARON AND DAN ARE GETTING A VERY CLEAR MESSAGE THAT PLAYING NICELY IS VALUED IN THEIR HOME. THEY ARE ALSO LEARNING ABOUT THE IMPORTANCE OF GOOD SIBLING RELATIONSHIPS.

Praising the child immediately for the desired behaviour is best, particularly when the child is quite little, as toddlers have short memories. Praising immediately helps the child to understand that the behaviour is valued. However, DELAYED PRAISE IS BETTER THAN NO PRAISE. Parents have busy lives and it is often later that a parent remembers how nice it was that the child complied. Tell the child: "Mohamed, it was lovely that you got ready for school on time this morning. I meant to say it to you at the time but I forgot as I was so busy. Thank you so much."

4. Rewards and encouragement

We all work for rewards. Ask yourself:

- Would you go to work and stay there for eight hours a day if there were no pay cheque coming later?
- Would you deny yourself an extra slice of your favourite cake, if you were not trying to maintain a healthy weight/lifestyle?
- Would you train on all those wet and cold evenings if you were not hoping to get your place on the team and bring home the cup?

Everything we do, or don't do, has a consequence. A REWARD is a positive consequence. We are ENCOURAGED to repeat behaviour if it brings a positive consequence.

> IF THE CHILD HAS TO WAIT FOR SUCCESS BEFORE SHE IS PRAISED, SUCCESS WILL BECOME MORE DIFFICULT FOR THE CHILD TO ACHIEVE AS SHE FEELS DISCOURAGED. HOWEVER, IF HER EFFORTS ARE PRAISED ALONG HER JOURNEY TOWARDS SUCCESS, SHE IS MORE LIKELY TO ACHIEVE SUCCESS. THE EXAMPLE BELOW ATTEMPTS TO ILLUSTRATE THIS.

Scenario 1

Tilly, aged eight, has been promised her favourite dessert after dinner if she gets all her spellings correct. She gets one wrong and therefore does not get her favourite dessert. Her parents may believe that this will spur Tilly on towards making a greater effort and getting all her spellings correct next time. It may do that but Tilly is clearly getting a message that nothing less than perfection will do. This can cause problems for Tilly now and later in life. However, it may do the reverse and discourage Tilly and she may feel 'it's too hard'. This approach has the potential to damage the relationship between Tilly and her parents.

Scenario 2

Tilly's parents have said they expect her to do well at her spelling test as she has practised them during the week. She gets six of the 10 correct and her parents says something like: "Good work, Tilly. You should be pleased with yourself, 60% is very good. You just got one letter wrong in the other four spellings. We can practise them again." Tilly's parents have focused on her success rather than her failure. Tilly will feel validated for her effort and encouraged to continue working on her spellings. The relationship between Tilly and her parents has been positively enhanced.

Even if Tilly never achieves 100% in her spelling test she will feel good about herself as she knows it is the effort that is important. Her attitude towards the challenges that life throws at her now and in the future is more likely to be one of healthy optimism rather than defeatist pessimism.

PARENTS OFTEN WORRY ABOUT THEIR CHILD'S HIGH AND UNREALISTIC EXPECTATIONS OF HIMSELF. THE CHILD GETS VERY UPSET WHEN HE DOES NOT ACHIEVE 100% ALL THE TIME. IF THIS IS THE CASE IN YOUR FAMILY, TAKE A FEW MINUTES TO CONSIDER WHETHER YOU ARE ENCOURAGING YOUR CHILD BY FOCUSING ON EFFORT OR DISCOURAGING YOUR CHILD BY FOCUSING ONLY ON RESULTS AND GIVING MORE ATTENTION TO FAILURE THAN TO SUCCESS.

Types of rewards

The most important reward a parent can give a child is positive attention and lots of it. As already outlined, a smile from the parent is very validating for the child.

Rewards such as a smile, an enthusiastic 'well done', a 'high five', a hug, and telling another important person in the child's life about his efforts and achievements cost nothing and are 'gold dust' in terms of building a child's self-esteem, and also building the positive relationship between parent and child. Rewards like these are often termed SOCIAL REWARDS. Every child and teenager responds positively to social rewards. Sometimes, this type of reward on its own is not sufficient to bring about the desired change of behaviour or to create a new positive habit. In these situations, MATERIAL REWARDS often provide the support needed.

Material rewards are rewards that can be measured in a more physical way. For instance, a new toy, money, etc. However, it is important to take a few minutes and think of what is most rewarding for your child. Each child is unique and what one child loves, another may not. However, it is very important to look first to rewards that don't have a monetary value as these are often the most rewarding for the child. They are also often the most accessible. Rewards such as:

- Extra play time;
- Extra TV time;
- Extra computer time;
- Cooking favourite dinner;
- Favourite dessert;
- Extra bedtime story;
- Allowed to stay up a little later at the weekend.

Note all the extras – this assumes that the parent is already having a play time with the child each day and reading a bedtime story each night.

Avoid big rewards that cost money, e.g. a new, expensive toy. These can be for very special occasions. For instance, if your child is having difficulty staying calm in frustrating situations you could come to an agreement with your child that each time you witness the child staying calm in a frustration situation he will earn 1 point. When he has X number of points earned he can trade them in for a monetary gift. Alternatively, your child could earn 20 cent each time he stays calm in a frustrating situation, and then he trades this in as he wishes. The point or 20 cent is an immediate reward, and the more of these the child earns the greater the ultimate reward. This is a very effective method for focusing a child towards changing a negative, and sometimes destructive, behavioural response to a more appropriate and safe one.

> HOWEVER, THIS APPROACH TO CHANGING BEHAVIOUR THROUGH REWARDS WORKS BETTER FOR OLDER CHILDREN WHO ARE ABLE TO UNDERSTAND THE IMMEDIATE REWARD AND ITS LINK TO THE LONGER-TERM, BIGGER REWARD.

The use of monetary rewards with teenagers has the additional benefit of exposing the teenager to the delight of delayed gratification. For example, the teenager wants a new item of clothing. The parent wants the teenager to practise good study skills. If the teenager spends two hours studying she earns one euro and when she has enough euros earned she buys the desired clothing. Ideally, the two hours studying will have become a habit by this time and the teenager will value her new item of clothing better for having earned and waited for it.

For younger children – children aged six and under – immediate rewards work best as the child's capacity for linking behaviour and longer-term rewards is limited.

> CHILDREN ARE DEVELOPING AND, UNLIKE ADULTS, IT IS EASY FOR THEM TO LOSE OLD HABITS AND DEVELOP NEW ONES. THEIR PERSONALITIES ARE FORMING – THE ADULTS' ARE FORMED. ADULTS CAN CHANGE BUT IT IS HARDER.

Rewarding the behaviour you want to encourage through positive attention and, if needed, a tangible reward, results in the child displaying this behaviour more frequently. A behaviour that is displayed more frequently becomes a habit and, as we all know, habits are hard to change. Never take a desired behaviour for granted. Give your child lots of praise for being successful at displaying this new behaviour regularly. Your specific reward system now concludes for this behaviour. However, if there is another behaviour your child is struggling to achieve you can create a new reward system for this other behaviour. Your child, having experienced success previously, will be motivated towards it again. SUCCESS BUILDS SUCCESS.

> A KEY PRINCIPLE HERE IS TO CONCENTRATE ON CHANGING ONE BEHAVIOUR AT A TIME. REWARD SYSTEMS OFTEN FAIL BECAUSE THERE IS MORE THAN ONE BEHAVIOUR INCLUDED IN THE REWARD SYSTEM.

KEY POINTS

- Present your best face to your child – the smiling one, the one that says 'I am happy to see you'. Present the face that gives your child a good feeling about you and him;
- Plan for play/special time with your child each day;
- Praise the behaviour you want repeated. Do not take any positive behaviour for granted;

- Reward your child's efforts;
- Focus on changing behaviour through a reward system for the behaviour you want instead of the negative consequences for the behaviour you want to eliminate;
- Each day, ensure your child gets more attention for *behaving* than she does for *misbehaving*.

2

Emotional development

Parents are usually very aware of the importance of their child's development in the social and academic areas. Unfortunately, they are not always as enlightened regarding the importance of emotional development. It could be argued that developing an awareness and understanding of our own and other people's emotions and feelings is the most important aspect of developing as a human being. Emotions are feelings that arise in the person in response to certain stimuli – external or internal. Such is the importance of emotions for survival and healthy development that the emotional memory system is thought to be present in some form at birth, unlike cognitive memory which develops from birth onwards. "We cannot remember things before the age of about three because until then the hippocampus – the brain nucleus that lays down conscious long-term memories – is not mature. Emotional memories, however, may be stored in the amygdala, a tiny nugget of deeply buried tissue that is probably functioning at birth."[4]

Parents are aware of the child developing language and proudly speak of the ever-increasing vocabulary of their child. The same awareness is not evident in relation to emotional vocabulary. Indeed, this is not surprising as when asked to name emotions, parents often struggle to name more than happy, sad, glad or mad.

The pre-verbal child communicates using vocalisations, gestures and eye movements. The emotional messages conveyed in these vocalisations are of great importance. A cry may say: "I am hungry." A smile may say: "I am happy." A giggle may say: "I am enjoying this"; and so on. The accompanying body language adds more meaning – flaying hands and feet while crying may communicate frustration; flaying hands and feet while giggling may communicate excitement.

> IF A SMALL CHILD CANNOT COMMUNICATE WITH WORDS, HE WILL COMMUNICATE IN SOME OTHER WAY AND OFTEN THIS 'OTHER WAY' IS TO USE BEHAVIOUR, E.G. THROWING THINGS, HITTING, BITING, ETC. IF THE CHILD HAS LANGUAGE AND KNOWS THE NAME FOR THE EMOTION HE IS FEELING, HE IS MORE LIKELY TO COMMUNICATE VERBALLY: "I AM ANGRY", "I AM SAD", "I AM AFRAID".

This chapter seeks to assist the reader in developing his own and his child's emotional vocabulary. The wonderful human ability to recognise and understand how actions and events impact the other person – EMPATHY – is discussed. The powerful effects of MODELLING (your child is learning from you at all times) and the role of TEMPERAMENT are also explored. The skills discussed and illustrated should give the reader a framework for supporting her child's emotional regulation.

Development of emotional vocabulary

Prior to the child reaching the toddler stage of development, parents are naturally gifted at emotion coaching. Have you noticed how, when bathing your infant and the infant is enjoying the experience, you often comment on this: "You love having your belly washed"; "You are enjoying the feeling of the water on your nose"; etc?

How often have you responded to your infant's smile with: "You are happy because..."

For some reason, or maybe many reasons – and it is not necessary to explore them – parents seem to stop this very important commentary when the child becomes a toddler and is starting to use words to communicate.

> Please continue to comment and name your child's emotions. It is vitally important for his emotional development. Do not judge emotions as good or bad. They are important messengers. Respecting them in yourself, your child and others ensures a happier future for all.

The following are some more tips for supporting the development of your child's emotional vocabulary:

- Improve *your* emotional vocabulary. You do this by becoming aware of how you are feeling at any given time and labelling that emotion. Do not be content with just deciding that you are happy or unhappy. Delve a little deeper and, if you decide that 'yes, I am happy', go one step further and ask yourself is 'happy' the best word to describe how you feel. Maybe 'content', 'satisfied', 'hopeful', 'safe', 'secure' or any other positive feeling might more accurately describe how you are feeling at that moment;

- Name the feeling you think your child is experiencing and why you think your child is feeling this way, e.g. "You are smiling, I think you are happy"; "You are sad, that is why you are crying." Be tentative in your assumptions. Only the child can confirm if you are correct in your assumption. Here is a little example to illustrate that very important point:

> Ellie, aged 13, is sitting at the kitchen table doing her homework. Ellie gets up abruptly from the table, pushing her chair back noisily in the process. She stomps out the door. Her mother, who was preparing dinner, follows Ellie into the hall and enquires as to what the matter is. Ellie replies in an angry voice: "Nothing". Her mother says: "Something must be the matter, Ellie, you seem very angry". Ellie shouts at her mother: "I am not angry!"

In this illustration, Ellie's mother reacted to Ellie's evident distress in an emotionally reflective way (she reflected to Ellie the emotion she thought Ellie was feeling – anger). However, Ellie has clearly told her (in an angry voice!) that she is wrong in her assumption. Many parents now focus on Ellie's angry response and berate her for shouting at her mother and, in so doing, miss a wonderful opportunity to build their relationship. A response that misses the opportunity of relationship growth would be something like: "Don't you shout at me, I am only trying to be helpful." A relationship-building response would be something like: "I can see something is wrong, Ellie, you seem upset." This statement is delivered in a kind voice and let hang in the air. Ellie may not immediately confide the cause of her upset to her mother. However, Ellie has learned that her mother is focused on her – Ellie's – feelings rather than her own. It is highly likely, almost certain, that Ellie will seek her mother out before long and confide what is upsetting her;

- Name the feelings you are experiencing yourself, e.g. "Mammy is very happy and that is why I am smiling"; "I hurt my finger, it is sore and now I feel a bit cross";
- Own your own feelings, e.g. "I feel annoyed when the toys are all over the sitting room floor." Never blame the other for your feelings. Never say: "You made me feel sad", "you make me angry". There is a simple truth to this – your feelings are *your* feelings, arising directly in you as a result of stimuli in your internal or external world. Nobody makes you feel anything. For instance, if I tell a joke to a group of friends, some will laugh because they find the joke funny, others might laugh out of politeness but not because they find the joke funny. Others don't find the joke funny and don't laugh. Everyone responds in his own unique way, depending on how the joke fits with his sense of humour.

Empathy

Empathy can be described as the ability to put yourself in another person's shoes and imagine how an event/situation/action *might* make you feel. It is not that you are feeling as the other person is feeling. It is instead an ability to imagine how you might feel if you were in that situation. A good example of a response that is not empathic was illustrated to the author in the following situation:

> A parent is bereft because of the tragic death of his daughter. Let's call that man Liam. A year later, his friend finds himself in a similar situation and says to Liam: "Now I know how you feel." Liam responds with: "No, you don't know how *I* feel! You know how *you* feel!"
>
> Liam's friend assumed he and Liam were feeling the same emotions because they both had suffered a similar bereavement. Liam very clearly sets him right. Had Liam's friend said to Liam: "Now I think I have some idea of what you are going through", Liam would probably have agreed with him – that he had some idea but not the complete picture.

Parents help the development of empathic feelings in their child by firstly MODELLING (see below) empathy for the child. When the child cries because another child has taken his toy, demonstrate empathy by acknowledging the child's feeling, e.g. "It's frustrating when Jake takes the toy you want."

Parents often make the mistake of thinking the way to teach the child empathy is by bringing the child's attention to how the other child is feeling. For instance, when the child tells the parent that he does not want to play with a peer, the parent's response often is: "Jake is sad because you won't play with him." This may make your child feel he is bad because he does not want to play with Jake and maybe he now plays reluctantly with Jake. However, it did not elicit any information as to why your child does not want to play with Jake in the first place. Alternatively, parents may try another approach, i.e. "How would you feel if he did not want to play with you?" While the child may say 'sad', this does not do anything to build empathy because the child's own emotions (which may be central to why he does not want to play with his peer) have been ignored.

The examples below relate to children aged anywhere between three and 10 years of age.

Example 1. Response without empathy

Child (Zac): "Ben won't play with me." (*crying*)

Mother: "Ben, play with Zac."

Ben: "I don't like Zac, I don't want to play with him!"

Mother: "Don't talk like that, Ben. Of course you like Zac, he is your friend."

(Ben may reluctantly play with Zac, but don't be surprised if a row breaks out again between the two boys.)

Example 2. Empathic response

Zac: "Ben won't play with me." (*crying*)

Mother: "Oh, that has upset you. Do you know why Ben won't play with you?"

Zac: "I don't."

Mother: "Let's ask him. Ben, Zac has a question for you."

(Mother may have to help Zac asking or he may ask by himself.)

Ben: "Zac wants to play the game his way, he never plays it my way."

Mother: "I can see that would be frustrating for you."

In example 2, mother responded with empathy towards both children. She has not issued demands or commands. Rather, she focused on what each child is feeling and what might have caused that feeling.

In the following examples, the first response is the one often used by parents. The second response is the more effective and certainly builds the positive relationship between parent and child as well as modelling empathy. We will also look at what the child has most likely learned from each response and how the child might feel.

Anna, teacher and mother

Child (Anna): "I hate teacher, she is so mean."

Mother (in a critical, frustrated voice): "What did you do now?"

Anna: "I did nothing, she just hates me."

Mother: "Teacher does not hate you, were you bold in class?"

Anna: "I did nothing."

Anna stomps off in a sulk.

What is the likely message Anna is getting from this response?

- Anna has learned that if she complains about teacher, she (Anna) is the one who did something wrong;
- Adults side with adults.

How might Anna feel?:

- She feels bad about herself;
- She feels her mother does not care enough for her;
- She feels hard done by;
- She feels angry and sad.

Empathic response

Anna: "I hate teacher, she's so mean."

Mother: "You sound angry. Tell me what happened."

Anna: "She made me sit by myself at the front of the class."

Mother: "I can imagine that did not feel nice. Have you any idea why she did that?"

Anna: "She said I was talking, but I only asked Kelsey for her rubber."

Mother: "It's not nice getting into trouble like that. Can you go back to your usual seat tomorrow?"

Anna: "Yeah, I think so."

Mother: "Ah, that's good. How can you make sure you don't get in trouble again?"

Anna: "I need to have my own rubber."

Mother: "Good idea. How about we put it in your pencil case now?"

What message is Anna likely to get from this response?

- Her mother will listen carefully to her;

- Her feelings are important;
- She has not been judged or blamed;
- Teacher has not been judged or blamed either;
- Her parent is interested in her and in what happens in school;
- There are little things she can remember to do and then she is less likely to get in trouble at school.

How might Anna feel?

- Good about herself;
- Happy again;
- Loved and cared for.

(The above is also an example of effective problem solving, which will be dealt with comprehensively in Chapter 6.)

Jessica and mother

> Jessica is 15 years old and her mother has just refused her request to go to the disco on Friday night.
>
> Jessica: "It's not fair. You and Dad are too mean. I am never allowed go anywhere. I f***ing *hate* living here."
>
> Mother: "Watch your mouth, young lady. That's an awful way to talk to your mother, and for that you will not be allowed to go to the Easter disco either!"
>
> Jessica slams the door and continues to harangue her mother on her way upstairs.

What message is Jessica likely to get from this response?

- Her mother and father are mean;
- She is never listened to;
- Different rules apply for her – when her mother is angry she often uses bad language but Jessica gets into trouble for the same thing (in my experience, if children use bad language, they have learned it from their parents);
- If you feel insulted, get angry and shout back.

How might Jessica feel?

- Angry;
- Sad;
- Hurt;
- Frustrated;
- Confused;
- Unloved.

Empathic response

Jessica: "It's not fair. You and Dad are too mean. I am never allowed go anywhere. I f***ing *hate* living here!"

Mother: "I know you are disappointed. However, the rule is one disco during term time. You were at the one that was held two weeks ago. You can go to the Easter disco."

Jessica: "It's just not fair. All my friends are going. Please can I go just this once and I won't ask to go next term. Please..."

Mother: "I know we seem very mean, Jessica, and it does make it harder when your friends are going. However, we are happy for you to go at Easter. The rule is one disco during term time."

Jessica leaves the room with a sulky look on her face, however she does not slam the door.

What are the likely messages for Jessica in this response?

- Staying calm and focused on the issue at hand is important;
- Her mother can be trusted to stick to an agreement;
- Her mother is a strong woman, not easily swayed by argument, emotion or protest;
- Her mother is fair and honourable.

How might Jessica feel following this response?

- She stills feels unhappy about not being allowed to go to the disco;
- Although she does not like mother right now, she respects her calmness and strength;
- She feels listened to and loved – although it will take a little while for her to consciously admit this.

(If Jessica continues to use bad language when angry or upset, her mother should deal with this at a time when both are calm.)

Key principle

A key principle for parents in relation to dealing effectively with disagreements between the parent and child or misbehaviours from the child is to stay CALM.

Parents readily admit to struggling with this in difficult situations. This is very understandable as parents are not robots but human beings with their own unique make-up and character traits. I am not a fan of giving lectures on how to stay calm – because I find other people's method of little value for me! Each parent is her own expert and, as such, knows what helps her to stay calm or return to a calm state.

Perhaps you have not given much thought to this before. Please do so now and make a list of the helpful strategies that you are already using but have not reflected on up to this point. For instance, remember the times when you 'kept a lid on it' in front of your boss, mother-in-law, father-in-law or other person whose behaviour was causing you considerable distress. What worked then? It may be the strategy for you to perfect.

The only rule is that your strategy or strategies for staying calm or returning to a calm state, must be safe for you and for you child. Please also remember that it is a work in progress and at first you will find changing your response difficult. The old adage of 'practice makes perfect' is true, and without realising it parents have often been practising an ineffective parenting response and now it is 'perfectly' ineffective! Start today and practise staying calm in frustrating situations. At times you will fail – you are human – and when you do apologise and move on. As you will see in the next section on 'modelling', doing the right thing after a wrong is modelling to your child how to right a wrong.

So be kind to yourself and have faith in your ability to STAY CALM.

Modelling

The parent is the child's first and most influential teacher. Children learn how to behave from watching how their parents behave in all situations.

It is interesting to hear parents complain of their child using bad language and when asked if anyone around the child uses similar language, the parent admits to having a habit of using bad language herself. Great credit is due to the parent for her honesty. And this is the first stage in correcting bad habits – owning up to them.

If you would like your child to speak politely, you must speak politely. If you would like your child to say 'please' and 'thank you', you must say 'please' and 'thank you'.

> IF YOU WOULD LIKE YOUR CHILD TO STAY CALM IN FRUSTRATING SITUATIONS, YOU MUST STAY CALM IN FRUSTRATING SITUATIONS.

This is called 'modelling' and is a key element in effective parenting.

If you want your child to be kind, caring, generous, tolerant and friendly, you must firstly demonstrate these skills to your child and then to others around you. Your child is absorbing what you say and what you do.

Finally, if you want your child to manage his emotions effectively, and this means expressing feelings through words rather than behaviours, you must model this behaviour yourself.

Temperament

Of course, your child has a temperament all of her own. Temperament can be defined as a way of behaving in the world that is innate rather than learned. We often refer to someone as being 'naturally easy going' or 'quick tempered'. Some children are placid, some are active, some are restless, some have very ready smiles while others appear sulky.

> However, it is vitally important to acknowledge that nurture, as in parenting style, can modify or intensify temperament.

Please remember that there are two sides to everything – good and not so good. A person who is easy to anger is often a person who has a heightened sense of justice. A person who gets upset easily is often someone of great sensitivity. A person who is very calm is sometimes slow to act.

It is very important to acknowledge useful aspects of the child's temperament type, while at the same time offering ways of managing problems that might occur because of temperament.

Key points

- Increase your emotional vocabulary;
- Identify and name for yourself how you are feeling in different situations;
- Name the feelings you think your child is experiencing from infancy, e.g. "You are smiling, you must be happy";
- Work on your empathy skills – which are an ability to understand how a particular situation or event may make another person feel – and remind yourself to be aware of how a situation or event might impact on your child's feelings. Be tentative, not definite, in sharing this with your child: "You look cross, could it be that you are feeling angry about that?";
- Behave towards your child in the manner in which you want your child to behave towards you and others – modelling;
- Look for the strengths in your child's temperament and acknowledge these to the child. If aspects of the child's temperament are causing problems, work with the child to find ways to manage these aspects so as to lessen their negative effects.

3

Social development

A socially competent person is one who is comfortable in the company of other people; has one or more close friends and is also part of a network of less close but companionable group or groups of people; has an ability to maintain good work relationships; and demonstrates reasonable levels of tolerance and understanding towards others. From birth, infants engage with the world and the people around them. They are social beings, but it is a very ego-centric sociability. The infant (and the toddler) reaches out to other people, she needs other people, but it is all about her needs and wants. If you watch toddlers under the age of three at play, you will see that, rather than being a cooperative process, it is a parallel process. The children play alongside each other rather than with each other. Cooperative play between young children is not present at birth but develops as the child grows.

As with every other area of child development, parents play a key role in facilitating the development of the skills necessary for the child to become a socially competent adult. These skills include: sharing; turn-taking; kindness; friendliness; helpfulness; manners; and patience. Children do not display these skills from birth. The infant and toddler's world is all about 'me, me, and me'. However, as these skills are integral to healthy development, happiness and indeed survival itself, the vast majority of children can learn these skills easily enough if the environment in which the child is growing and developing facilitates this learning. For a small number of children, particularly children with autism spectrum disorder (ASD), acquiring these skills is more difficult and requires knowledge and understanding on the part of parents, teachers and others. ASD, by definition, is a social and communication disorder, hence the child will experience significant challenges in everyday social interaction.

(For more information on this, please see the list of excellent books, websites and organisations in the Appendix.)

Facilitating social skills development

The EFFECTIVE PARENT facilitates and teaches social competency skills in their child by naming the desired skills and praising the child's efforts at using them. Social skills training should start in infancy. When spoon-feeding your infant, create sharing/turn-taking moments, e.g. "A spoonful for baby and a spoonful for dolly/mammy/teddy/daddy", etc. As your baby grows from an infant to a toddler to a pre-schooler, facilitate social skills development as often as possible, as demonstrated in the following scenario.

> Aoife and Katie, both aged three, are playing together at Aoife's house. Aoife's mother is doing her chores in the room where the children are playing. She looks up every few minutes with comments such as:
>
> "It's so lovely to see you both playing so nicely together."
>
> "Aoife, you are so kind, sharing your toys with your friend. That is a really friendly thing to do."

Notice how Aoife's mother named and praised the behaviours – playing nicely, kindness, sharing, friendliness – that she is witnessing between the children. This is called SOCIAL COACHING.

It is very interesting to notice the child's reaction to this social coaching, which is as simple as the parent just commenting on and naming the behaviour she sees. Almost without fail, the child will continue to share, etc., in order to earn more of this positive attention.

> CHILDREN LOVE POSITIVE ATTENTION AND THRIVE ON IT.

The child is learning that certain behaviours are valued and get the sort of attention that gives the child a nice feeling. Therefore, the child will repeat this behaviour.

> WHAT GETS ATTENTION GROWS AND DEVELOPS, WHAT IS IGNORED WITHERS AND DIES.

Of course, sharing, turn-taking and being friendly do not always come easily to a child. Here are some examples of this. In the first scenario, the mother deals ineffectively with the situation and in the second she deals with it effectively.

Scenario 1. Ineffective parenting

> Tom and Aaron, aged five and four, respectively, are playing with some building blocks in Tom's home. Tom's mother is busy in the kitchen when she hears a cry from the sitting room. She runs in to find Aaron crying because Tom refuses to share the block Aaron wants.
>
> Mother: "Tom, give that piece to Aaron. Don't be so mean. He came here to play with you and you must share with him. Also, he is younger than you."
>
> Tom: "He's a baby, that's all he is... and I don't want to play with him."
>
> Mother: "Don't be bold, Tom. You have to play with him. How would you like it if he did not play with you?"
>
> Tom's mother goes over to Aaron and says: "Let's find another piece that you can play with. Tom is being bold." Aaron is happy to do this but Tom is not and is now looking very sulky and out of sorts.

What is the possible learning for Tom from this interaction?

- That he is bold – which is a bad thing to be;
- He has done something wrong;
- His mother is cross with him;
- Aaron got him in trouble.

How might Tom feel?

- Bad about himself;
- Misunderstood;
- Confused;
- Angry;
- Dislike of Aaron because he is involved in all this bad feeling.

Aaron learns that Tom is bold and that crying gets you what you want. However, Aaron may not feel good about this because his friend Tom is upset and this does not feel good to him.

Scenario 2. Effective parenting

> Tom and Aaron, aged five and four, respectively, are playing with some building blocks in Tom's home. Tom's mother is busy in the kitchen when she hears a cry from the sitting room. She runs in to find Aaron crying because Tom refuses to share the block Aaron wants.
>
> Mother: "What's the matter Aaron, why are you crying?"

Aaron: "Tom won't give me..." pointing to the building block he wants.

Mother: "Oh, I see. It's tough when you both want the same piece. Did you ask Tom?"

Aaron: "He won't give it..."

Mother: "Maybe if you asked him if you can have it when he is finished with it... Tom, how long more do you need that piece for?"

It is very likely now that Tom will hand over the piece, or at least indicate when he will hand it over. If he says he needs it for the next hour, you can gently say something like: "That's a long time for Aaron to wait, Tom. How about we say five minutes? Have you any ideas for the best piece for Aaron to play with in the meantime?"

It is very likely now that Tom will get involved in finding another piece for Aaron. Tom's mother now has an opportunity to praise Aaron for waiting and Tom for helpfulness.

How might Tom feel when the situation is addressed as above?

- Understood;
- Good about himself and about Aaron;
- Happy to share.

What might he have learned?

- Sharing brings good feelings;
- Helping also brings good feelings.

What possible learning is there for Aaron?

- To ask for what he wants;
- It is possible to find something else to play with while waiting.

How might Aaron feel?

- Happy again;
- Good about himself and about Tom.

Notice how Mum stayed calm and focused on coaching the behaviour she wants to see more of. This is not always easy, given the demands that parents may be facing at any one time – household chores, stress, tiredness.

> However, dealing calmly and effectively with this situation now will bring more peace to your home and gain time for you in the longer run as the children learn to play nicely together.

The ego-centric nature of the child, and the biological fact that young children have shorter attention spans than older children and adults, makes sharing, turn-taking and waiting difficult for the child. The parent and teacher have the very important role of helping the child to learn this skill. Unfortunately, the strategies used are often ineffective and rows break out between the children. It is common for parents, and sometimes teachers, to *demand* that the child shares or turn-takes. Threats are also often used, e.g. "If you don't give that toy to Oscar right now, you will have to stand in the 'bold corner'." This often results in the child sharing but doing so very reluctantly. This attitude of parents and teachers definitely leads to bad feelings in the child and, momentarily at least, damages the relationship. (Don't despair, relationships are damaged and repaired all the time, but what we really want is less damage and more building of a positive relationship.)

I recently had the pleasure of baby-sitting three relatives aged three, seven and nine years old. All are the most beautiful and delightful girls it is possible to encounter. The seven-year-old finds it a little more difficult to wait her turn. Life is so exciting for her she wants to experience what everyone else is enjoying *right now*! This, very understandably, annoys her more patient sisters. A small trampoline in the garden was providing great fun but only one child at a time could safely play on it. So a system had to be devised to make playing on the trampoline continue to be a source of enjoyment rather than a contentious play thing. The dialogue went something like this:

> Me: "Girls, we have one trampoline and three girls. Only one can play on it at a time. Who is going to go first?"
>
> Girls: "Me, me, me..."
>
> Me (to self: silly, of course they would all want to go

> first, quick thought... hmmm): "Ok, of course you all want to go first. Ok, ok... Who will go third?
>
> Three-year-old: *"Meeee!"*
>
> Me: "Oh, you are so good. That is so wonderful that you are going to let your sisters on before you... Wow! I am really impressed."
>
> Seven-year-old: "I'll go second... E—— can go first."
>
> Me: "You are super, that is fantastic sharing. Now to decide how long each person gets on the trampoline?"
>
> Seven-year-old (looking at a big clock in the kitchen): "Let's time it."
>
> The clock was then used to time each person on the trampoline. As the other two waited their turn, counting down with the clock provided a distraction, as did a chair they enjoy sitting in.

The main point in this story is that it was a collaborative process – the children were involved in the decisions. Also, note that the nine-year-old child was less vocal in the process because she is older and was better able to watch the process evolve than to jump in too hastily. As a result, she got to use the trampoline first! Please note also that the children were not provided with the toy and expected to play with it. The parent, or babysitter in this instance, needed to support the children in 'sharing', 'playing nicely' and, most importantly, having fun.

When parents are exposed to these contrasting strategies, the responses often vary as follows:

- "Ah, come on – you'd have to be perfect to be the parent in the effective scenario' (*thinking – this is not the real world*);
- "That's fine if you had lots of time" (*thinking – I am too busy, give me a quicker fix*);
- "If that was my child he'd have punched the other child before I could get there" (*thinking – these are perfect children and my child is not!*);
- "Oh God! Now I see where I am going wrong" (*thinking – I have damaged my child*);
- "Ah – light bulb!" (*thinking – now I know what I have to do differently*).

As stated in Chapter 2, changing your response is never easy, but you can do it! You are already on that journey because you are reading this book. A fact that should help you is the often quoted definition of insanity – expecting change while doing everything in the same way.

As also stated in the last chapter, 'practice makes perfect'. Practise these new skills at every opportunity. When parents, who say it takes too much time to do things differently, utilise these skills they are pleasantly surprised to find that parenting effectively takes less time than the ineffective alternative.

Finally, and perhaps most importantly, perfection – in the way we understand it, getting everything right – does not exist in parenting. As the name of this book states, EFFECTIVE is the key word and concept. Nature does not get things right all the time. If it did we would live in the perfect climate with the perfect people – ugh!

> THE AIM IS TO GET IT RIGHT ABOUT 70% OF THE TIME. IF YOU HAVE BEEN GETTING IT WRONG ABOUT 70% OR MORE OF THE TIME, DON'T WORRY. IT'S STARTING THE JOURNEY TODAY TOWARDS BECOMING AN EFFECTIVE PARENT THAT MATTERS.

KEY POINTS

- Model social skills for your infant, toddler, school-age child and teenager. This means you are aware of being kind, patient, caring, considerate and compassionate at all times (you are allowed to make a mistake sometimes! But remember to acknowledge your mistake and in so doing you are truly demonstrating EFFECTIVE PARENTING);

- Model social skills for your infant, toddler, school-age child and teenager by sharing willingly, by speaking politely, by taking turns;

- Remember, your child has to learn social skills. You are your child's first and most important teacher. Look for opportunities and there will be many every day to TEACH SOCIAL SKILLS;

- Involve your child in deciding how to manage situations that lead to conflict. This is the beginning of 'problem solving', which is the cognitive process of finding an effective solution to a problem, and is the subject of Chapter 6.

4

Academic development

Academic development can be described as the child's growing ability to acquire, store and use knowledge. As with all other areas of a child's learning, the child's parents are his primary teachers.

It is often said that the child's developing brain absorbs information in the same way that a sponge absorbs water. Parents are often astonished at the knowledge their very young child displays. A three-year-old child of my acquaintance, on observing an older relative smoking a cigarette, asked: "Why do you smoke?" The relative was a bit lost for an explanation and said: "I will give them up tomorrow." When the three-year-old came upon the same relative smoking the next day, she asked: "Why are you *still* smoking?" The remarkable memory and logic of the child often confounds adults!

Providing an environment that is rich in new experiences greatly aids the cognitive development of your child. International studies provide evidence for the many benefits associated with learning more than one language.[5] So if your home is blessed with fluency in two languages, ensure your child is exposed to and encouraged to develop fluency in both.

As well as discussing your role in your child's academic development, this chapter also explores the formal educational system – school – and how you can support your child in making school a happy place where your child can succeed academically.

Supporting your child's learning

Parents are prone to asking a lot of questions of the young child, in the mistaken belief that this is the best way to teach the child about the world around her. Asking a child questions can be useful if the child knows the answer and gets praise for her knowledge. However, if the child does not know the answer it can lead to confusion and doubt in the child about her own abilities.

The best way to facilitate knowledge growth in your young child is to use DESCRIPTIVE COMMENTS rather than questions. So, instead of asking "what colour is that?" and then correcting the child if he gets it wrong, make comments such as "that is a red block" or "you are using a red block".

Parents are excellent at using descriptive comments with their infant. Remember when your child was an infant in your arms and almost all of your communication involved describing your infant's emotions, facial expressions and actions? On occasion, you described your actions also. The communication between you and your infant probably involved statements such as:

> "Look at you... with your smiley face!"

"You are smiling at Daddy!"

"You are taking it all in, looking all around you."

"You are wondering what Mammy is doing. I am making your food."

"Oh, you love having your nappy off... you love the feeling of being free of the nappy and you are kicking your legs with delight."

However, parents often change from comments to questions when the child becomes verbal.

There is so much your child can learn from your descriptive comments. Here are some ideas of what to comment on:

- Objects – "that is a car";
- Colours – "the car is red, a red car";
- Quantity – "you have two spoons";
- Actions – "you are putting the red brick on the blue brick";
- Feelings – "you look so happy playing with your doll" ;
- Relationships – "cup and saucer go together", "a spoon is great for scooping up the porridge";
- Manners – "you remembered to say please – well done!";
- Friendship – "you and Sarah are great friends, you have great fun together."

Questions

Questions in themselves are not wrong and often necessary.

The way of asking the questions can be very important.

Closed questions are questions which generally get a 'yes', 'no' or 'I don't know' answer. Examples are:

> "Do you like school?"
>
> "Why are you sad?"
>
> "Are you happy?"
>
> "Is she your best friend?"
>
> "May I have a piece, please?"
>
> "Did Dad make your dinner today?"
>
> "Why were you fighting with him?"
>
> "Did you enjoy your holidays?"

The opposite to a closed question is an open question. Open questions are ideal for situations in which exploration of a subject is required. If you want more than a 'yes' or 'no' answer to the situations being enquired about above, try some of the following:

> "Tell me what you like about school."
>
> "What do you dislike about school?"

"Please tell me what is making you sad."

"What brought that lovely big smile to your face?"

"Who is your best friend?"

"When can I have a piece?"

"What did Dad make for dinner today?"

"How exactly did that fight start between you two?"

"What was the best part of your holiday?"

"What would make you feel better right now?"

Let's use an example to illustrate the points above regarding closed and open questions. Patryk, aged 10, has told his father he hates school.

Ineffective parenting response

Dad: "Why do you hate school?"

Patryk: "I don't know, I just do..."

Dad: "No one likes school, you just have to make the best of it."

Effective parenting response

Dad: "What do you hate about school, Patryk?"

Patryk: "I hate teacher, he is always picking on me."

Dad: "Oh, I am sorry to hear that. Tell me more..."

Patryk: "He is an idiot and he is very mean."

Dad: "Hmmm, I can see you don't like him very much..."

Patryk: "No, I don't like him at all... I hate him... I wish Mr S was our teacher – he is nice."

Dad: "When you say he picks on you, Patryk, what do you mean?"

NOTICE DAD HAS NOT CONTRADICTED PATRYK OR REPRIMANDED HIM FOR CALLING HIS TEACHER AN 'IDIOT'. INSTEAD, PATRYK'S DAD HAS ASKED AN OPEN QUESTION BEGINNING WITH 'WHAT' AND HE HAS CONTINUED TO LISTEN TO WHAT PATRYK IS SAYING WITHOUT JUDGEMENT.

The dialogue between Patryk and his Dad is continuing rather than being closed down, as in the previous ineffective response. This is called problem solving and is the subject of Chapter 6. We will return to this scenario there.

Reading and academic development

Reading to and with your child has many advantages:

- It should, in the first instance, be enjoyable and therefore is an excellent relationship-building opportunity;
- Books contain knowledge. When presented with new information in an exciting and engaging way, children soak it up;
- Books present new ideas to the reader. The child's developing brain loves new ideas and the opportunity to discuss these brings true wisdom;
- Reading books with your child helps language development. Children who are exposed to books and reading at a tender age have superior vocabularies to their peers who have not been exposed to books and reading;
- Reading with your child provides an excellent opportunity for increasing emotional vocabulary, empathy and awareness of other perspectives by discussing the story from the perspectives of all the characters.

Read to and with your child. Have books in your house – the libraries have lots of books to lend. You can use any material that has pictures and words on it. In fact, for very young children, pictures on their own are enough. Build stories around the pictures. Invite the child to suggest what might happen next...

Have a bedtime routine of story time. Allow the child to choose the story, which will *be read when the child is in bed.* Five or ten minutes is sufficient reading time. Let the child know beforehand how long you will read for. For instance, a good indicator other than time can be 'one story only'. If you want to acknowledge an achievement or effort of your child you could reward it with an extra story. For instance: "Abdul, because you helped your sister with her homework this evening, I am going to read you an extra story tonight."

School and your child

The vast majority of parents make the decision to have their children formally educated in the group setting of school. A major change in Irish society over the past 30 or so years is the growth in pre-school education. As a result of this, starting school for children is not the wrench from home that it could be if the child has not been in a group setting without a parent before. However, there is a major difference in formal schooling and pre-schooling. Pre-school is relaxed: there are rules, but children have more freedom to choose an activity and to move around the classroom. Learning in pre-school is play based. The pre-school classroom generally has smaller numbers of children, and greater adult-to-child ratios. The primary school setting is a formal one, there are considerably more children, most of whom are older, bigger and more experienced than your child, if he is just starting. There is just one teacher in the classroom (there may be a special needs assistant but she has responsibility for a specific child). There is a curriculum to be followed and the rules are more stringent than at pre-school.

In Ireland, the law states that a child can enter the primary school system at age four and must have started primary school by six years of age.[6] It is common for Irish children to start at age four and a half. I am personally not in favour of children starting formal education until at least age five. I have yet to encounter a parent who has regretted starting their child at primary school at age five, but I have met many who regret starting the child at age four. If you do start your child at age four, remember your child will share the classroom environment with some children who are one year older. As each day of a young child's early life heralds in new developments, it could disadvantage your child to be sharing classroom space with children who find adhering to rules, and expectations etc easier. The Australian psychologist, Steve Biddulph, author of the excellent book, *Raising Boys*, discusses this in the 2018 updated edition of his book.[7]

The following are some tips to help make school a happy place for your child:

- Seriously consider age five as the age at which your child starts formal schooling;
- Visit the school, chat to the principal and vice-principal. Ask about the ethos and the code of conduct. Do all of this before your child starts school;
- Do your best to talk to other parents whose children attend the school, in order to get an idea of what the school might be like for your child;
- It is vitally important that you develop a positive, supportive relationship with your child's teacher. She or he is likely to be the most important person after you in your child's life;
- Take an active part in the school community activities, volunteering for extracurricular activities, joining the parents' council, etc.

Homework

This can be a contentious issue. Some say it is of little or no value. I like the notion of homework and believe it to be of value in consolidating new information that the child has encountered during the school day. I also believe it is a good habit to develop. The old adage, 'no gain without pain', has at least some truth. Homework provides a discipline of using time to better oneself in terms of knowledge and skills.

It is very important to note that homework is a *contract* between the child and the teacher. Teacher gives the homework, the child does it and presents it to the teacher and the teacher evaluates it.

The parent's role in homework is to provide a suitable quiet space for the child to complete it. Having a house rule that supports engaging in homework is good practice, such as: *homework first... then leisure time* (more of this in the next chapter). The parent's role also involves ensuring the child only spends the recommended time on the homework. Talk to the teacher or check the homework journal to find out the maximum time your child is to spend on homework each evening. There are clear recommendations around this. If your child is taking longer than the recommended time, talk to the teacher. Maybe the teacher is expecting too much of the children or maybe your child struggles a little bit more than might be expected. If homework becomes a fraught issue for your child, it is your responsibility to correct this.

> A child will not learn if stressed. No child should be unduly stressed by homework or school work. If homework is too

CHALLENGING FOR THE CHILD, HER SCHOOL EXPERIENCES WILL NOT BE HAPPY ONES. HAVING A HAPPY SCHOOL EXPERIENCE IS THE NO. 1 PRIORITY.

Resist the temptation to correct the homework. This is the teacher's job. It is also the teacher's job to provide a discipline measure for the child to encourage compliance with homework tasks. For instance, if a child does not do the homework as expected (and the homework given was reasonable), the appropriate discipline to encourage future compliance is to keep the child in at play time to complete the homework.

Resist the temptation to do the homework for the child! I know of one parent (an adoring foster Dad), who did such good colouring for his foster daughter that teacher sent him home *his own page* to colour!

Key points

- Comment on your child's environment rather than ask questions about the environment;
- Questions in themselves can be very important. However, focus more on questions that explore rather than close down conversation;
- Have books in your house. Remember, the libraries are full of great books for children and usually free to borrow;

- When buying a present for your child, or any child, consider buying a book;
- Read to and with your child from babyhood;
- Consider starting your child in primary school at five rather than four years of age;
- Ensure that school is a happy, supportive environment where your child can learn;
- Build a supportive and positive relationship with your child's teacher(s);
- Consider volunteering in the school community;
- Ensure homework consolidates learning rather than stresses your child. This is achieved by:
- Having and enforcing a rule such as homework first... then leisure time
- Ensuring your child is not spending longer than the recommended time on the homework assignments
- If your child is struggling to complete the assignments, have a chat with the teacher as she may be expecting too much
- Stay calm and resist the temptation to do the home-

work for your child!

- Do not expect perfection
- Remember, it is the teacher's job to correct the work.

5

Rules and limits

We all need rules. If there were no rules, there would be chaos. Imagine there were no rules at work outlining employers' and employees' expectations and obligations, or no traffic rules to ensure we walk, cycle and drive safely. We would not have the ability to imagine for long as, without work, the economy would collapse and, without rules on the road, there would be deaths and, eventually, with both coming together, annihilation. Yes, that sounds a little extreme; but it highlights an essential point – if there are no rules and boundaries within the family unit, the unit will not survive and the individuals within will live limited and compromised lives.

Children need rules and boundaries. Rules are, firstly, about safety; secondly, about order; and, finally, about respect for oneself and others. So have a few rules in the home that are clearly stated and firmly adhered to.

Your role as a parent is to *firmly* but *kindly* ensure the rules are adhered to.

This chapter focuses on household rules and appropriate boundaries. Supporting your child in adhering to the rules, by applying NATURAL and LOGICAL consequences, is discussed. Finally, the very important but often misunderstood difference between DISCIPLINE and PUNISHMENT is explored.

ESTABLISHING HOUSEHOLD RULES

As stated in Chapter 3, children comply best when they are involved in the process of making the rules. It is recommended that you sit down with the child/children and discuss the rules that will make your house a safe and happy place for all who live there. You, as the parent, will take the lead in the discussion. However, the children must have a say, too, and, please remember, some rules apply to all who live in the home. For instance, having a rule of *speaking politely* applies to you, too!

When establishing the rules for your house the following principle is very important:

> STATE THE RULES IN A POSITIVE WAY, E.G. 'HOMEWORK FIRST, THEN PLAY TIME,' RATHER THAN 'NO PLAY UNTIL HOMEWORK IS DONE'.

EXAMPLES OF HOUSEHOLD RULES

Pre-schoolers

- Ask politely for what I want, i.e. say "Please may I have";
- Play nicely, e.g. share my toys.

School age

- Ready for school at 8.30am;
- Homework before play time;

- Bedtime is 8pm;
- Play nicely, e.g. share, take turns;
- Use nice talk – "please may I have";
- Screen time for up to one hour a day (this includes TV).

Teenagers

- Ready for school at...
- Unless there are extra-curricular activities, come straight home after school;
- Homework before leisure, e.g. screens, socialising;
- Bedtime on school days at 9pm, at weekends 10.30pm;
- Screens can be used for up to two hours per day;
- Rooms tidied at weekend.

These are just guidelines – each home makes the rules that best suit their family circumstances. If you did not have specific rules up to now, it may be best to start with two or three and build on them as required.

> If a particular behaviour becomes an issue in your house, building a positive rule around it could be a great way of encouraging the opposite behaviour. For instance, if two siblings are going through a stage of fighting a lot, an appropriate rule to introduce would be: 'kind words, hands and feet in our home.'

If one child starts to fight – and both will forget the rule at times – gently remind with: "Oops, you forgot the rule, remember... kind words, hands and feet in our home." This gentle but firm reminder is often enough to bring the siblings back on track. Remember to praise immediately if the child complies. If the child does not comply and is intent on continuing the fight with her sibling, you need to intervene more firmly to stop any hurt that could ensue. Praising the child who has not engaged in the fight and re-directing the other child, or having the offending child take a 'time out' (because time out is a contentious issue it will be explained in detail in Part 2), is an effective parenting practice. If both children are offending, separating and re-directing both, or having both take a time out, is appropriate.

Natural and logical consequences

Notice in the guidelines above that the sanction for not keeping the rule is part of the rule. For instance: *homework before leisure time...* implies the child is not allowed to play, watch TV, etc until he has first done his homework. The effective parent ensures this rule is adhered to.

Effective parenting is about being *firm* and *kind*. If something unexpected happens, e.g. there is an electrical outage, the effective parent writes a note in the journal the following day to explain why the child does not have the homework done. However, if there is no unexpected event and the child refuses to do any homework the effective parent does not write a note excusing the child. He *firmly* and *kindly* reminds the child of the rule. He does not get cross with the child but ensures, as far as is practical, that the child does not involve himself in any leisure activities until the homework is done.

These situations present great opportunities for effectively using strategies discussed in previous chapters. For instance, using empathy as discussed in Chapter 2 – "I know homework can be a bore..." – demonstrates to the child that you are looking at this from his point of view. Even if this does not result in the homework being done, it certainly contributes in a positive way to the relationship between you and the child. If the child persists in refusing to do homework, the parent can write a note in the journal informing the teacher of the child's refusal to do the homework. These scenarios will be dealt with in more detail in Part 2 of this book.

When I ask a parent what the consequences of a particular action are for a child, the reply, often, is 'none'. However, when the parent is asked to reflect for a moment he realises that 'no consequence' is in fact a consequence – the consequence of getting away with it! Consequences can be either NATURAL or LOGICAL.

NATURAL CONSEQUENCES happen naturally, without any intervention. For instance, not eating usually results in feeling hungry; wearing insufficient clothing results in feeling cold; going out in the rain without any head cover or umbrella means my hair will get wet, etc.

LOGICAL CONSEQUENCES are sanctions that are put in place to ensure compliance with a rule or law. As already stated, driving my car over the speed limits means a fine and penalty points *if I am caught!*

Examples of supporting the child in making good choices by allowing natural consequences are:

- If the child refuses to eat the food presented, the parent does not insist on the child eating. However, the child is given the clear CHOICE of *eat* or *go hungry*. When applying this rule be mindful of individual taste. Taste buds are individual and all of us have a food we hate. Do not force a child to eat something he hates. However, be sensible. Encourage the child to try all foods and resist the temptation to give in to the child's demands for special food. You are being an INEFFECTIVE PARENT if you find yourself making special dinners for different family members. The old adage of 'hunger is good sauce' is actually true. Except in very limited and specific circumstances – children with sensory challenges sometimes have difficulty with certain foods (see Part 2 for some tips on how to manage this) – the feeling of hunger sooner rather than later overcomes the resistance to eating;

- If your child refuses to put on her coat when going out to play, do not insist on her putting on her coat. When she gets cold she will come in and ask for her coat. Resist insisting to your child that he will be cold – you don't know this. In certain circumstances, a logical consequence may be appropriate here. For instance, a child insisting on playing in the rain without wellingtons. The rule of *if you play in a puddle you must wear your wellies* encourages compliance. The LOGICAL CONSEQUENCE if the child refuses to wear wellies is: she is not allowed to play in the puddle.

USE NATURAL RATHER THAN LOGICAL CONSEQUENCES IN GENERAL. HOWEVER, NEVER ALLOW A NATURAL CONSEQUENCE THAT IS NOT *SAFE*. IT

IS SAFE TO LET YOUR CHILD EXPERIENCE HUNGER, COLD, WET, ETC. IT IS NEVER SAFE TO ALLOW YOUR CHILD TO INJURE HIMSELF OR RISK INJURY TO HIMSELF IN ORDER TO LEARN.

Examples of applying logical consequences in EFFECTIVE PARENTING are:

- The child refuses to go to bed on time, the child misses the bedtime story *or* goes to bed earlier tomorrow night;
- The child comes home at 5.30pm instead of 5pm. Tomorrow evening the child comes home at 4.30pm. If the child comes home late again, she stays home the next evening. On the following evening she is allowed out again but reminded that you trust she will be home at the agreed time. If she is late again, she stays in for two evenings. The principle here is that the sanction is FAIR, IS RELATED TO THE MISBEHAVIOUR AND ENCOURAGES THE DESIRED BEHAVIOUR;
- The child refuses to do a chore, he is not allowed to engage in leisure activities, i.e. watch TV/screens, play with toys or friends, etc., until he has completed the chore.

Children will test the rules. This is completely normal. We all test rules. How often have you driven your car at excess speed? If you got a speeding fine you are very likely to keep within the speed limit, for a time at least. Rules without sanctions do not work. It is normal to keep rules because we dislike the sanction. Rules are about safety and so the important thing is *keeping* the rules, not necessarily *why* we keep the rule. However, there is a caveat to this. In some families, there is a very harsh punishment regime for the child when he breaks the rules. This can lead to the child feeling hard done by. The child keeps the rules out of fear of the parents' overreaction. This approach damages the relationship. Furthermore, this approach, used to excess, can encourage passive aggressive defiance in the child or teenager. Examples of this can be: the child/teenager *lying* to and about you; the child/teenager *losing* some item that is important to you; the child/teenager *forgetting* to do something that was of importance to you.

> CHILDREN LIKE TO BE SAFE AND SECURE. THEY LIKE TO KNOW WHAT IS EXPECTED OF THEM. WHEN OFFERED A CHOICE THE CHILD IS MUCH MORE LIKELY TO CHOOSE THE BEST OPTION. WHEN THE CHILD UNDERSTANDS THAT THE RULES ARE ABOUT SAFETY AND RESPECT (FOR THEMSELVES AND OTHERS), THEY ARE MORE LIKELY TO KEEP THEM.

DISCIPLINE VS. PUNISHMENT

The terms DISCIPLINE and PUNISHMENT are often used as if they are the same thing. THEY ARE NOT.

The following exercise should prove this to the reader:

> Get an A4 sheet of paper. Draw a line down the middle. Write DISCIPLINE on one side and PUNISHMENT on the

> other. Now, under PUNISHMENT write all the words/ thoughts that come to your mind. Don't think too much about this, just write whatever comes to mind. Then do the same with DISCIPLINE. Use one word to sum up what you have written under PUNISHMENT. Do the same with DISCIPLINE – use one word to sum up.

Is it possible that the word *hurt (physical or emotional)* describes best what you have written under 'punishment'?

Is it also possible that the word *respect* adequately sums up what you have written under 'discipline'?

It is vitally important to understand the difference in those two terms.

> PUNISHMENT NEGATIVELY IMPACTS THE PARENT-CHILD RELATIONSHIP. DISCIPLINE BUILDS A POSITIVE RELATIONSHIP BETWEEN PARENT AND CHILD.

You are at risk of veering onto the punishment side of insisting on compliance with a rule or demanding compliance when you are angry.

A clash of wills often arises between a parent and child. It can often be over something quite simple – the parent insisting on the child wearing warmer clothing because the *parent* tells the child: "You will be cold." The child, who is not cold, or maybe a teenager or approaching teenage years, when appearance is important, refuses to wear the article of clothing. The parent views the child's resistance as cheekiness and demands compliance. The child digs her heels in and the parent gets angry and imposes a severe sanction for the 'misbehaviour'. Here is an example to illustrate this point:

> Kayleigh, aged 14, is just about to exit the house for school on a cold Friday morning. Her mother notices that she is not wearing her coat.
>
> Mother: "Kayleigh, it's freezing out there, you will get your death of cold. Please put on your coat."
>
> Kayleigh: "I am not cold. I don't need a coat."
>
> Mother: "Please put on your coat. You are just over a bad cold and rain is promised later."
>
> Kayleigh ignores her mother and opens the door to leave...
>
> Mother (now angry): "Come back here, Kayleigh! If you don't wear your coat you will be grounded for the weekend."

Kayleigh may now sulkily comply because her mother is angry and/or because she does not want to be grounded. Or Kayleigh may leave for school banging the door behind her, leaving her mother in an angry and frustrated state. Either way, the interaction above and the bad feelings that ensued could have been avoided if Kayleigh's mother had used the following EFFECTIVE PARENTING strategy:

Mother: "Kayleigh! Are you forgetting your coat?"

Kayleigh: "I don't need it."

Mother: "It's a very cold morning Kayleigh and rain is forecast for later..."

Kayleigh: "I'll be fine."

Mother: "I am worried that you are just over a bad cold and you will get sick again."

Kayleigh: "I hate that coat, it makes me look like a wuss..."

Mother: "Hmmm... I see. Has somebody said something?"

Kayleigh: "No, I just hate it..."

Mother: "Is there a compromise here, Kayleigh? I can't afford to buy you a new coat yet. Would you consider taking the coat with you, and if you are cold or it rains maybe putting it on?"

Kayleigh: "Oh... Okay."

Or maybe Kayleigh still refuses to take her coat. Take a moment to reflect and it will become clear why one approach is EFFECTIVE and the other INEFFECTIVE...

In the first instance, Kayleigh's mother's initial instruction to Kayleigh sounds like genuine concern for her daughter's health. However, when Kayleigh does not share her mother's opinion and refuses to wear her coat, her mother quickly moves into a power-struggle mode by demanding that Kayleigh do as she requests. The most important issue now is Kayleigh's compliance, not her health. When Kayleigh refuses, she becomes angry and frustrated. She is possibly thinking Kayleigh is difficult or is becoming difficult. Kayleigh also becomes angry and defiant. Her opinion has not been sought on why she does not want to wear her coat on a cold morning, so neither her mother nor the reader can be sure why this is so. What we can be sure of is that Kayleigh's feeling towards her mother will be on the negative side after this exchange and, if it rains or she feels cold, she won't have the protection of a coat.

In the second instance, Kayleigh's mother stayed calm, honest and respectful. She did not get into a power struggle with Kayleigh. Instead, she enquired as to why Kayleigh does not want to wear her coat. When she hears that Kayleigh hates her coat, she neither gives out nor gives in. Instead, she informs Kayleigh that she cannot afford to buy her a new coat just yet and asks Kayleigh if she would consider taking the coat with her in case she changes her mind. In all likelihood Kayleigh will do this, as she will appreciate her mother's calm concern and her understanding of why she does not want to wear the coat. Even if she still refuses to bring the coat with her, the relationship between mother and daughter will have been built upon rather than fractured. Her mother has made a request, suggested a compromise and, ultimately, respects Kayleigh's choice.

> GIVING CHILDREN CHOICES IS THE EFFECTIVE PARENTING WAY OF AVOIDING RELATIONSHIP-DAMAGING POWER STRUGGLES.

Do not personalise your child's defiance. Your child's refusal to do something is *not* about you, as demonstrated above. It is about your child and her opinions and feelings.

Because Kayleigh defied her mother in the first example, her mother became angry and frustrated and threatened to ground Kayleigh for the weekend. When she calms down she may regret having lost her temper and may feel that grounding Kayleigh is too punitive or difficult to implement. Reflecting on behaviour and taking corrective action is right and proper and a great opportunity to model *humility* and how to right a wrong for your child. However, sometimes the parent adopts an ineffective approach rather than an effective parenting approach. The following example attempts to illustrate this.

> On Monday evening, Susie, aged nine, who was playing with her friends on the street outside her home, did not come in for dinner at the agreed time of 6pm. She ignored her mother when she called her in. Her mother called her in for a second time and this time she said she was coming in. However, Susie still did not come in. It was not until her mother went on to the street and shouted at Susie and told her she was now grounded for a week that Susie came in. Her mother is now angry.

> Mother (in an angry and loud voice): "Susie, you are

very bold. Why can you never come in when I call you? You are now grounded for the rest the week."

Ineffective parenting approach

Later on, when Susie's mother has calmed down, she feels guilty about shouting at Susie. She also realises that grounding her for a week is harsh and will be hard to implement. So she calls Susie aside.

Mother: "Susie, I am sorry for shouting at you but if you came in on time I would not have had to shout. You can go out tomorrow but you must come in at 6pm; if not, you will be grounded for a week."

What is the possible learning for Susie?

- Her mother is sorry but she – Susie – is responsible for her mother's feelings and behaviour;
- Her mother is not serious about applying sanctions;
- Her mother attempts to control Susie's behaviour by threats.

How might Susie feel?

- She feels bad about making her mother angry;
- She feels bad about herself – she upsets others;
- She feels resentful about being blamed for her mother's shouting behaviour.

Effective parenting approach

> Later on, when Susie's mother has calmed down, she realises that grounding for a week is harsh and that grounding for one day would be far more appropriate. She also realises that Susie is more likely to keep the rule of coming in on time, and when called, if the sanction is fair and if she is given an opportunity to do the right thing soon after. So she calls Susie aside and says the following:
>
> Mother: "Susie, I was very cross a little while back when it took three calls from me for you to come in. Because of that I was too harsh with the sanction. I am sorry for that and for shouting. You will stay in tomorrow evening and you cannot have any friends in to play. You can go out to play the following evening. I am confident that you will remember to be in by 6pm then." A smile and a hug end this exchange.

What might Susie have learned?

- Mum is serious about the rules being adhered to;
- Mum is human and makes mistakes;
- When a person makes a mistake it is important to take corrective action.

How might Susie feel?

- Susie is pleased that her mother has apologised for her behaviour, which had made Susie feel bad;
- Susie feels happy again and resolves to keep the rule

regarding being in by 6pm in future.

There is a third approach that parents need to protect against here also. That is OVERCOMPENSATION.

A parent who loses his temper easily is also often a parent who suffers guilty feelings shortly afterwards. In the previous example, this would be something like the following:

> Mother: "Susie, I am very sorry for shouting at you like that. I did not mean to upset you. If you had come in on time none of this would have happened. I feel awful when I shout at you, you know that, don't you? You must do as you are told, otherwise Dad and I get very upset and you don't want that, do you? You are not grounded but you will be if this keeps happening. You can have an extra piece of apple tart after dinner to make up for me shouting at you. I hate it when we fight."

What might Susie have learned?

- Her mother is sorry for her inappropriate behaviour but it is Susie's fault. Susie is responsible for her parents' feelings and actions;
- Sanctions for misbehaviour do not apply if her mother over-reacts;
- Her mother's feelings are more important than Susie learning to do the right thing.

How might Susie feel?

- Susie feels confused regarding the rules and whether she needs to keep them or not;

- She feels somewhat resentful for being blamed for her mother's actions and feelings.

Key points

- State your rules so your child knows what is expected rather than what is forbidden – "We use polite language at all times" rather than "No cursing";
- Have consequences that are fair and fit the misbehaviour – e.g. "Come in earlier tomorrow evening or stay in if you do not come in on time this evening";
- Support the child in making appropriate choices by allowing the child experience the natural consequence of an action if it is safe. Otherwise, apply the logical consequence;
- State your rule in such a way that the sanction is included – e.g. "Homework before TV/leisure time";
- Increase your awareness of what constitutes DISCIPLINE and what constitutes PUNISHMENT. Aim to never use punishment, as it damages the relationship between you and your child. Discipline builds a positive relationship and gains your child's respect;
- The stance you adopt in establishing and maintaining rules is of vital importance. A firm and kind stance

builds a respectful relationship with your child. A strict and severe stance damages the relationship and, while the rules may be kept, the child often does so out of fear.

FINALLY, REMEMBER YOU ARE HUMAN. YOU WILL MAKE MISTAKES. THE IMPORTANT THING IS TO ACCEPT RESPONSIBILITY FOR MISTAKES, APOLOGISE AND MOVE ON.

6

Problem solving

We all encounter problems on a regular basis, from the very minor (having no eggs when an omelette is fancied) to the major (being made redundant from the job that pays the bills). Good problem-solving skills are essential for a healthy and happy life, and lucky is the child whose parents facilitate this.

However, parents are often ineffective in helping their children become good problem solvers. I believe one of the reasons for this is the parents' emotional enmeshment with their child.

It often breaks a parent's heart to see their child upset and the parent's urge is to immediately make the child feel better.

> The parent then sets about solving the child's problem rather than helping the child build the skills to solve her own problems.

In so doing, the parent is often giving a message of: "You can't solve this problem, it is too big for you, and only I can solve it." The child could also be getting a message of: "It's not ok to experience negative feelings, immediate return to positive feelings is essential." And so the opportunity for giving the child an essential life skill is, at best, compromised or, at worst, lost.

It could be argued that EFFECTIVE PARENTING *is* supporting the development of EFFECTIVE PROBLEM-SOLVING SKILLS in the child.

Chapter 1 is about BUILDING POSITIVE RELATIONSHIPS. The skills discussed there are applicable to all relationships right throughout life.

In facilitating the EMOTIONAL DEVELOPMENT of the child, the parent is supporting the development of EMPATHY SKILLS, EFFECTIVE LISTENING SKILLS and EMOTIONAL REGULATION SKILLS. This forms the discussion in Chapter 2.

The parent's role in the development of the SOCIAL SKILLS necessary for living in the world happily with others is discussed in Chapter 3.

Chapter 4 guides the parents towards ensuring the development of the child's ACADEMIC POTENTIAL.

Supporting the child to become a respectful and disciplined individual and member of society through the establishment and maintenance of APPROPRIATE RULES AND BOUNDARIES provides the material for Chapter 5.

As will be illustrated in this chapter, EFFECTIVE PROBLEM SOLVING brings together most, and sometimes all, of these skills when the parent is supporting the child in finding a solution to a specific problem.

Facilitating the development of Effective Problem-Solving Skills

A key question for the parent to keep in mind is:

> How do I want my closest family/friends to respond when I have a problem?

Adults almost always respond to this question with: "I want her to listen, I don't want to be told what to do."

Now, ask yourself: Have you listened to your child without interruption, as your child told you of some difficulty he was *having* or *causing*? If you did interrupt, was it to:

- Gain more clarity about the situation?
- Give advice?
- Tell the child what to do?
- Make a judgement on your child or the other child/person?
- Admonish your child?

I strongly suspect that the reader is answering yes to at least some of the questions above. Be very proud of yourself if you answer 'yes' to the first question. Keep reading if you answer yes to some, if not all, of the other questions and be proud of yourself for doing so! It is not always easy to admit, even to ourselves – "Oops, I got that wrong." But it is always brave and honourable. Furthermore, it proves that you have *humility* and I believe this to be a wonderful but undervalued human attribute.

Formula for problem solving

Having a formula for problem solving is a good idea. On first use, it may seem a little staged. However, as with everything else, the more you use this formula the more natural it will become and soon you will use it without thinking.

This is the formula I advocate:

- Empathy – acknowledge the problem and the feelings that may be associated;
- Ask what has happened;
- Listen to the child's explanation – do not interrupt, unless it is for clarification;
- Ask what the child has done to try to solve the problem himself? Did it work? Praise the child's effort;
- Avoid 'why' questions or closed questions, as outlined in Chapter 4, because they often lead to 'yes', 'no' or 'I don't know' answers, which do not offer much in the way of progress. Questions starting with 'what', 'when', 'where', 'how' or 'who' usually lead to more conversation and exploration.

For example, if your child is complaining because her friend won't play with her and you ask, "Why won't she play with you?", she is likely to say: "I don't know."

If you ask: "What was she doing when she refused to play with you?" she is more likely to give a fuller answer and one that leads to more information as to why this has happened: "She was playing with Zofia."

- If the child's way of solving the problem worked and it was a safe solution – no one got hurt and there are no negative feelings – that is great. Congratulate the child and move on;

- If the child's solution did not work, acknowledge the child's effort and ask what other ideas the child has that might be useful;
- Resist the temptation to offer *your solutions*. If your child is struggling with identifying possible solutions, respectfully ask the child for permission to suggest one. Then suggest one, and do so tentatively, as you will see in the illustrations below. The rationale for this is simple: suggesting a solution that the child has not thought of enables the child to process and think of other possible solutions;
- Make a list, either written or oral, of all possible solutions and, one by one, the ones that are not likely to work can be eliminated with the simple question: "What would happen if...?"
- Agree the solution that is most likely to be useful, and suggest the child try it, and report back on the result;
- Sometimes it is a good idea to role play with your child a possible solution. This can give confidence and also identify any problems that may arise. These can then be worked through;
- Finalise this piece of work by having a play session or a nice cup of something warm and soothing with the child as a reward for the good work you have done together;
- Check with the child if he tried the solution and if it worked. If not, go back to the drawing board and go through the process again.

More often than not, your child will be able to solve the problem himself by using the agreed solution from the formula above. Sometimes, you will need to involve yourself more actively in the solution. However, never do anything without the child's knowledge and agreement. Some tips will be given on how to secure the agreement of a reluctant child later in this chapter.

Example

In Chapter 4, Patryk, aged 10, tells his Dad that he hates school. Of note, most children dislike school! It only becomes a problem if the hatred of school is affecting the child's behaviour or mood. In extreme cases, a child may refuse to go to school. A child may also cry each night before bed because he dreads the thought of having to face school in the morning. The reasons for this can be many and varied and are sometimes more about the parent than about the child, e.g. a child who is worried that something bad will happen to his parent while he is at school.

By listening and using open questions, Dad discovers that Patryk hates his teacher (not school; he said he would like to have Mr S as his teacher) because his teacher is "always picking on me". Mindful of the problem-solving formula, Dad asks...

> Dad: "When you say he picks on you, Patryk, what do you mean? (*Seeking clarity.*)
>
> Patryk: "I can do nothing... he is always on at me..."

Dad: "Can you give me an example of his 'picking on you'?" (*Staying on task and seeking a concrete example.*)

Patryk: "I can't. I don't know and you will only give out to me anyway..."

Dad: "Patryk, I am very glad you are telling me this. It is important that you tell me or someone you trust when you are unhappy about something... I want school to be a nice experience for you." (*Reassuring Patryk that he is there to support him and not to criticise him. Confirming the importance of telling someone if upset.*)

Patryk: " If I ask Darren for his rubber, he gives out to me. He made me sit out all of PE today."

Dad: "I know you love PE. That would have been hard for you. What happened that he did that?" (*Dad uses empathy and asks another open question to gain more information.*)

Patryk: "We were just jumping around, but I was the only one who got into trouble."

Dad: "You feel he singles you out?" (*Dad demonstrating he understands.*)

Patryk: "He always does that, and then the others tease me for getting in trouble."

Dad (puts his arm around Patryk): "Hmmm, that's not very nice... and is causing you to hate school." (*More empathy and physical consolation.*)

Patryk (now tearful): "I suppose I still have to go there..."

Dad: "You do, but it does not have to be so horrible for you. Have you any idea of what would make this better?" (*Dad is firm but kind, and moves to helping Patryk find a solution.*)

Patryk: "Maybe I do talk a bit too much... School can be so boring at times."

Dad: "Yes, that is true. There are 29 other boys and girls in the class so it must be hard for a teacher to keep everyone's interest at all times. But I like your idea of talking less. Is there anything else that would help you to get on better with Mr M?" (*In a very seamless manner Dad has also empathised with teacher's difficult job of managing a classroom of 30 children, while also praising Patryk's idea for a solution.*)

Patryk: "I don't know. Mr S is a much nicer teacher. He is sound. He gives his class free days off homework. Mr M never does that."

Dad: "It's true Patryk, we all have favourite teachers. I can remember mine. How about you practise talking only when it's allowed in class and see how you get on then? If you are still unhappy we will have another chat and see what we can do." (*Dad suggests Patryk use his solution – it is the solution Dad would also have chosen! – and, very importantly, says they will review progress.*)

Patryk: "Ok..."

Dad: "Now, how about a game of draughts?"

Patryk: "Cool."

Notice Dad did not make any negative judgement of Patryk's behaviour or of the teacher's action. Instead, he focused on understanding the issues involved by using empathy and open questions. Patryk will feel listened to and understood. He has accepted responsibility for his behaviour and has decided to correct it. Very importantly, Dad will review progress with Patryk and, if Patryk is still having difficulties either managing his own behaviour or in his relationship with the teacher, Dad will sit down with Patryk and go through the process again and agree on another plan. The next plan might involve Dad talking to the teacher, but this will only happen with Patryk's consent and full knowledge. Patryk may be involved in the discussion if he wishes.

Follow-up (a)

Dad is reviewing the plan with Patryk three days later.

Dad: "Patryk, how are you getting on with Mr M now?"

Patryk: "I am being very good and I have only got in trouble once for talking."

Dad: "Well done, Patryk. You should be very proud of yourself. Keep it up."

(No need for further action. Dad will check in regularly with Patryk about school and continue to praise his efforts at keeping the classroom rule.)

Follow-up (b)

Dad is reviewing the plan with Patryk three days later.

Dad: "Patryk, how are you getting along with Mr M now?"

Patryk: "He is still picking on me..."

Dad: "I am sorry to hear that. Are you managing to keep the rule around talking out of turn?"(*Sympathy and appropriate question.*)

Patryk: "I am. But every time there is any noise in the class he looks straight at me and says he knows who is causing the disruption."

Dad: "That sounds very unfair. What do you think we should do next?" (*Empathy and very important question that gives a clear message of 'us' rather than just Patryk having to find a solution.*)

Patryk: "Nothing, there is nothing I can do. He just hates me!"

Dad: "You sound very upset about this, Patryk. Can I suggest something?" (*Empathy and respectful request.*)

Patryk: "Yeah..."

Dad: "Maybe I should have a chat with him."

Patryk: "Oh no, that would only make things worse!"

Dad: "What would happen if I spoke to him?"(*Exploratory open question.*)

Patryk: "He'd hate me more and I would be slagged at school and called a baby 'cause you spoke to him."

Dad: "Patryk, I am really sorry that this is happening to you. You should be very proud of yourself for talking to me about it and also for trying to solve this yourself. Sometimes, adults, parents and teachers, need to be reminded that the child has the right to feel comfortable in school. I think I know a way that I could speak to the teacher, with you present if you like, and without your classmates knowing I have spoken to him." (*Sympathy, praise, encouragement, support.*)

Patryk: "How would you do that?"

Dad: "I would ring him and ask for an appointment. I would also make very clear to him in the conversation that he is not to mention in the classroom or to the other children that I am meeting with him. This is a private meeting."

Patryk: "Yeah, but you would be seen in the school."

Dad: "I am going to have to ask him to meet me after the children have left for the day or in the principal's office or some other office away from the classroom."

Patryk: "You will still be seen and I will get slagged."

Dad: "It really bothers you, how your classmates might react?" (*Picking up on Patryk's concerns and asking an open question.*)

Patryk: "Tom L and Aaron M and their gang are always slagging everyone. They made Joseph cry the other day."

Dad: "That sounds nasty." (*Giving a name to the behaviour outlined above.*)

Patryk: "They are nasty."

Dad: "Is Mr M aware of how those boys behave?" (*Dad resists the temptation of applying the label 'nasty' to the other boys and instead explores if the teacher is aware of their behaviour.*)

Patryk: "I don't think he cares. And the funny thing is, when Tom L was teasing Caitlin in the class the other day, it was Caitlin who got in trouble."

Dad: "I am really glad you are telling me this, Patryk. It sounds quite serious. Every child should feel safe in school. I am going to have to talk to the teacher and maybe Mrs C, the principal, about this. However, I need to do it in a way that you feel confident that nothing will get worse for you. How about I ring Mr M and ask for a meeting after school? I will tell him it is serious and I need to meet with him when there are no children around." (*Reiterating the importance of confiding, naming the seriousness of the issue, and also stating a very important right – that a child feels safe in school. Dad then advances a plan to be discussed and agreed.*)

Patryk: "What will you say to him?"

Dad: "If you like, you can come with me? I will say to him that you are not very happy at school at the moment and that you have confided some worrying things to me. I will say that you feel picked on and that some other boys are intimidating children in the class." (*Dad respectfully invites Patryk to be there if wants to be, and is clear on what he will say.*)

Patryk: "I don't want to go with you. But promise you

will tell me what he says. And make sure you go at a time that no one sees you."

Dad: "I certainly will, Patryk. The most important person here is you. School should be and can be a happy place. It's my job as your parent to do all I can to ensure that. It's surprising how things change when we challenge the person or people whose behaviour is upsetting us." (*Reiterates message of Patryk's happiness being paramount and Dad's own duties regarding this.*)

Patryk: "I hope so."

Dad: "I have 20 minutes to spare now. How about we have a kick around in the garden?"

Patryk: "I'll get the ball..."

Patryk has obeyed the school rule but is still getting in trouble. Dad empathises with Patryk and, through further open questions, discovers that Patryk is being treated unfairly by his teacher. He also discovers that the 'teasing' and 'bullying' type behaviour of some children in the class is causing a problem for other children and could cause a problem for Patryk. Dad realises that this is a problem Patryk cannot solve without the intervention of an adult. Dad then discusses with Patryk how he (Dad) can help resolve this problem without Patryk feeling further exposed and anxious.

Never go behind the child's back. To do so will negatively interfere with the trust between you and the child. Maintaining the child's trust in his parent/guardian is an essential element in keeping the child safe.

Key points

- All the strategies and skills discussed in the five preceding chapters have a part to play in effective problem solving;
- Your role is not to solve your child's problem. Your role is to support your child in developing the skills necessary to solve his own problem;
- Sometimes, your child needs you to take a more active role in the solving a problem as demonstrated in *Follow up (b)* above. Only do so if the problem is too big for the child to solve without an active intervention by you;
- Praise your child's effort to solve the problem prior to involving you. We learn by trying and failing and then trying a new strategy. This takes courage, which deserves big praise;

- Offer no judgement of your child's ideas or efforts. Instead, ask the simple question: "Did that make things better?"

PART 2

Introduction to Part 2

When parents seek help in relation to a child's behaviour, it is usually in relation to a specific issue that the parents are struggling to manage.

The first issue discussed in Part 2 of this book is ATTENTION. The rationale for discussing the concept of attention first is that POSITIVE ATTENTION from the parent to the child is fundamental to all positive behaviour change. It is my experience that behavioural issues in a typically developing child inevitably involve some level of negative attention from the parent. This is perfectly understandable. The impulse when a child misbehaves is for the parent to 'get cross'. However, again in my experience, this usually does not help to change the misbehaviour. The following mantra is a good one to keep in mind when raising a child:

> IF WHAT YOU ARE DOING WORKS AND BUILDS A POSITIVE RELATIONSHIP BETWEEN YOU AND YOUR CHILD, KEEP DOING IT.
>
> IF WHAT YOU ARE DOING WORKS BUT FRACTURES THE RELATIONSHIP BETWEEN YOU AND YOUR

CHILD, YOU NEED TO CHANGE IT.

IF WHAT YOU ARE DOING DOES NOT WORK, YOU NEED TO CHANGE IT.

The other issues dealt with in Part 2 of this book are as follows:

- Tantrums;
- Biting;
- Mealtimes and food issues;
- Bedtime;
- Bullying;
- Children fighting and time out;
- Refusing to do as told;
- Anxiety.

7

Attention

The phrase, "he is doing it for attention", is often uttered in relation to a child's misbehaviour. To just leave it there, with no attempt to understand the concept of ATTENTION, does the child a huge disservice and can be damaging. So, let's consider attention.

The *Oxford Dictionary* defines attention as: (1) notice taken of someone or something; the regarding of someone or something as interesting or important; (2) the action of dealing with or taking special care of someone or something.[8]

Attention can be either 'positive' or 'negative'.

POSITIVE ATTENTION can be defined as engaging with your child, verbally or behaviourally, in a manner that makes your child feel good about himself and about you. Very importantly, it is the building block of a positive relationship between you and your child. Examples of giving your child positive attention are: praising your child; smiling at your child; engaging in a pleasant conversation with your child; respectfully listening to your child; showing concern for your child: and soothing your child when he is upset.

NEGATIVE ATTENTION can be defined as engaging with your child in a manner that makes your child feel bad about himself and about you. Examples of this are: criticising your child; shouting at your child; scowling at your child; punishing your child rather than facilitating appropriate behaviour through positive discipline; arguing with your child; and issuing negative commands to your child, e.g. "Stop whingeing", "stop fighting", "stop being bold".

Consider the following. If a baby's entrance into the world has been without complications, the first thing the baby does is cry. Now, imagine for a moment that the baby is left on the delivery table and everyone – mother, father, doctor, nurses, etc. – abandon the baby. What happens? The baby will cry... nobody comes... the baby stops crying... nobody comes... the baby cries again... still nobody responds. Eventually, what will happen if the baby is left unattended for a day, two days, three days...? Yes, the baby will die. This is a stark example but one which I hope will illuminate the essential point that your child cannot tolerate 'no attention' because attention is fundamental to survival. And, for this reason, every human being has an innate drive for attention. So, if your child is not getting sufficient attention from you when he is *behaving* as opposed to *misbehaving*, he will revert to misbehaviour because one thing is sure – he will now get attention!

Positive attention is best

Negative attention is second best

Because

YOUR CHILD CANNOT TOLERATE *NO ATTENTION*. IF HE IS AN INFANT IT *WILL* RESULT IN DEATH AND IF HE IS AN OLDER CHILD IT *COULD* RESULT IN DEATH.

How often have you found yourself taking the opportunity to do work or enjoy time to yourself when your child is happily and quietly engaged in some activity? It is perfectly understandable that, as parents, we all do, or have done, that. However, if your pattern is to ignore your child completely during this time, and to give attention when your child demands your time and attention or misbehaves, you are, in fact, encouraging your child to expect a response to his demands or misbehaviour. The solution to this is simple:

NEVER IGNORE THE BEHAVIOUR YOU WANT TO ENCOURAGE IN YOUR CHILD.

So, for instance, when your child is happily engaged in some activity, notice her with any of the following:

- Gentle pat on the head;
- Smile;
- A few words of praise – "great to see you concentrating so well", "enjoying your favourite programme", "having fun with your friend", "playing nicely", etc.

The reason parents don't do this is also simple: they are afraid it will encourage the child to seek more attention. Initially, it may do so, because this is good attention and the child thrives on good attention. However, as you become better at noticing your child when he or she is behaving – being good – and ignoring demands for attention, the child will engage more in the behaviour that gets noticed and less in the behaviour that is ignored.

> PARENTS READILY ADMIT THAT MISBEHAVIOUR TAKES CONSIDERABLY MORE OF THE PARENTS' TIME AND ENERGY (USUALLY NEGATIVE) THAN NOTICING THE 'GOOD' BEHAVIOUR.

For misbehaviour such as siblings or friends quarrelling, give attention in a positive way, such as reminding the children that they can play nicely. For instance: "Children! I see you are forgetting your nice behaviour. It can be hard to play nicely all the time, but I bet you can make a good attempt." Then notice, praise and perhaps reward the effort: "Well done. It makes for a happy home when we are nice to each other. I think I will make pizza for dinner tonight."

The inattentive, easily distracted and impulsive child

As was stated in Part 1, Chapter 2, each individual has his own unique temperament. Some children will be calm, relaxed, easygoing and thoughtful. Other children will be easily distracted and prone to inattention. If you are the parent of an inattentive and easily distracted child it can make your parenting job more difficult. On the other hand, it can have advantages. For instance, the easily distracted child is also easily distracted out of misbehaviour and redirected into appropriate behaviour, whereas the more attentive child might also be the child who is prone to sulk and not as easy to redirect. Also, the easily distracted and impulsive child tends to be more energetic. Harvesting this energy and coaching the child towards the positive use of this energy could lead to great success in terms of career later in life.

A common mistake made by parents of 'busy' children is that they constantly correct the child. In other words, the child is constantly told 'don't do' and rarely told 'do' instead. The following scenario will illustrate this common mistake and the consequences that can accrue when a parent continues to react as outlined.

Ineffective parenting response

> Jakub, aged 7, is a busy child. He likes to be outdoors and when indoors he goes from one activity to another at speed. Just now he has snatched the TV control from his brother and has changed the channel. His brother is not happy and complains to his Dad.
>
> Dad: "Jakub, don't do that. Give that control back to your brother."
>
> Jakub throws the control at his brother and snatches a pencil from his sister, who has been drawing quietly at the kitchen table. She is not happy.
>
> Dad: "Jakub, what did I tell you! Do not grab things

> from anyone. Go upstairs to your room and don't come down until I call you!"
>
> Jakub grumbles but goes upstairs. On the way, he stumbles on the stairs and makes a lot of noise.
>
> Dad: "Jakub, stop making that racket!"

What has Jakub learned?

- That he must not grab from anyone;
- That he gets in trouble for grabbing;
- That he must stop making a racket.

These are all very useful things to learn. However, Jakub's Dad will be even more frustrated when Jakub continues to grab items from his siblings. Jakub's Dad may feel hopeless about changing his son's behaviour. This behaviour continues because what Jakub has not learned is:

- What to do instead of grabbing something that takes his interest;
- How to wait patiently;
- How to make less noise.

If Dad continues to respond to Jakub in this way, the situation will not improve and, in all likelihood, will get worse. As the situation worsens, so also will Jakub's feeling about himself. He is most likely to view himself as:

- Someone who never gets it right;
- Someone who is always in trouble;
- Someone who upsets other people.

His self-esteem will suffer. He may also feel:

- Sad;
- Hard done by;
- Confused;
- Angry.

> Because he is not experiencing empathy for his impulsivity, his empathy skills may suffer and, instead of feeling sorrow for those whom he has upset, he may feel annoyance or even anger.

Using effective parenting techniques Jakub can be supported towards managing his challenging behaviour in a more appropriate way.

Effective parenting response

> Jakub, aged 7, is a busy child. He likes to be outdoors and when indoors he goes from one activity to another at speed. Just now he has snatched the TV control from his brother and has changed the channel. His brother is not happy and complains to his Dad.
>
> Dad: "Jakub, come here!" Dad ensures he has Jakub's full attention before continuing.
>
> "What is the right thing to do when you want something that someone else has?"

Jakub: "I ask for it."

Dad: "Yes that is right. So..."

If Jakub now gives the remote back to his brother, Dad will thank him for that and coach him further towards asking instead of grabbing. However, if Jakub throws the remote at this brother, which he is likely to do because of his impulsivity, Dad will continue along the following lines using behaviour and language similar to below.

Firstly, Dad will take Jakub by the hand or arm (this is to still him and to ensure he is attending). Dad will then take the remote control and, handing it to Jakub, say something like...

Dad: "Jakub, give it back to your brother using your polite manners please..." (*We are assuming here that Dad has previously coached Jakub about what 'polite manners' look like, i.e. asking politely, waiting patiently and saying thank you. If not, he will have to spend some time doing so now and will take Jakub to another room to do it as it would be unfair to further interrupt his brother's leisure time.)*

If Jakub now politely gives the remote back to his brother, Dad will continue...

Dad: "That's good, Jakub. Now, what do you do when

you want something that someone else has?"

Jakub: "Ask..."

Dad: "'Please may I have...' Say this to your brother now, Jakub."

Jakub's brother may accede to Jakub's request or may say no. If he says yes, Dad will encourage Jakub to thank him and Dad will also acknowledge his sharing. If he says no...

Dad: "Your brother is still watching his programme, Jakub, what will you do in the meantime while you wait your turn?"

The advantage of easily distracted and impulsive children is that they quickly turn their attention to something else. However, Dad needs to guide and support this, otherwise it might be that Jakub grabs the pencil from his sister.

Dad also needs to acknowledge that it can be difficult for Jakub to wait his turn and to ask rather than grab. So, Dad says something like...

Dad: "Jakub, I know it can be difficult to wait one's turn. I also know that you are working hard on this and getting better at asking rather than grabbing. Be proud of yourself."

Setting up a reward system, as explained in Chapter 1, to encourage 'waiting' and 'patience' in Jakub, would also be a very good idea. Each time Dad sees Jakub appropriately asking or waiting his turn, he will praise him and tell him he has earned 1 point. When Jakub has earned 10 points he gets a no-cost reward that he likes, such as extra rough and tumble play with Dad.

Five minutes of play for 10 points and 10 minutes of play for 20 points. This is just a suggestion. The key principle here is that Jakub is being rewarded for controlling his impulses, which means he will continue to work hard at this. Also, Dad is paying attention to Jakub's efforts and successes rather than his failures.

Possible learnings for Jakub:

- He can pay attention;
- He can control his impulses;
- He can do the right thing;
- He forgets sometimes but Dad is helping him to remember;
- When he wants something he needs to ask for it;
- Finding something else to do while waiting helps him to be patient.

How might he feel?

- Good about himself;
- Good about Dad, who helps him get things right;
- Loved;
- Happy;
- Proud when he remembers to wait, to pay attention and to control his impulsivity.

Key points

- Attention is vital for survival and your child needs it – in fact, you need it too. How long would you survive on your own on a desert island?

- Ensure your child is getting lots of positive attention – a simple smile is gold dust;

- Remind your child of the positive choice she can make, rather than threaten with a negative consequence;

- Never take good or desired behaviour for granted. Always notice it, which is a reward in itself. Sometimes give a more tangible reward, such as the child's favourite dinner, dessert, an extra story, extra playtime or some small thing the child likes;

- Ignore annoying behaviour.

Please keep the concept of attention and its importance for human survival in mind as you raise healthy, happy and effectively parented children.

8

TANTRUMS AND MELTDOWNS

Toddlers are prone to having 'tantrums' from time to time. It is important to distinguish between a TANTRUM and a MELTDOWN.

A small child can get worked up and show the behaviour we call a TANTRUM, e.g. crying, screaming, flailing hands, flailing feet, when some desire of the child is refused by the parent. In other words, the child wants to play with a particular toy and the parent says: "No, you cannot play with that toy right now, you have to have dinner first." If displaying this behaviour gets the child what she wants, e.g. the parent gives in and lets the child play with the toy, the child has learned that this behaviour gets her what she wants and she will do it again.

A MELTDOWN can look very like a tantrum, e.g. crying, screaming, flailing hands, flailing feet; *however,* the underlying cause is fundamentally different. A child has a meltdown when something in his environment provokes an intense fear or when she suffers a sensory overload. The child is not misbehaving out of a desire to have a 'want' met but is instead having a meltdown to try and have a 'need' met. The need may be to feel safe again, or to be protected from the sensory overload.

Tantrums

Ineffective parenting response(s)

Ella is three and a half years old and does not want to stop playing with her toys.

> Mother: "Ella, it's time to put your toys away and have dinner."
>
> Ella: "I don't want dinner, I want to play."
>
> Mother: "No, Ella. It's dinner time and the toys must be put away."
>
> Ella ignores her mother and continues to play.
>
> Mother (in an angry voice): "Ella, I told you to put those toys away. Put them away right now."
>
> Ella (in a whiney voice): "No, I want to play."
>
> Mother: "Stop being so bold, Ella, and do what you are told right now."
>
> Ella continues to whine and to play.
>
> Her mother goes over and takes the toy from Ella's hand. Ella starts to scream and throws herself on the floor screaming and kicking.

Some parents would now give out to Ella for 'being bold' and 'behaving badly'. Other parents would try to coax Ella out of the tantrum. Other parents would ignore the tantrum and only give Ella attention again when she ceased 'tantruming'. However, the attention given then often is negative attention in which the parent gives out to Ella for 'being bold' and 'not doing as asked in the first place'. Or perhaps some parents would give in to Ella's tantrum and give the toy back to her.

The possible learning for Ella in any of the above situations might be:

- She is a bold and difficult child;
- Having a tantrum gets attention – sometimes nice attention and, more often, negative attention. PARENTS! REMEMBER: WHAT GETS ATTENTION WILL BE REPEATED;
- Her mother is cross and does not love her;
- This is how to get what she wants.

How might Ella feel?

- Angry;
- Even though she may get her own way it does not feel good;
- Confused;
- Unloved;
- Sad.

Effective parenting response(s)

> Mother: "Ella, in three minutes it will be time to put the toys away and to have dinner." (*Ella is made aware*

that in a short time she will have to stop playing because it is dinner time.)

Ella: "Ok."

Mother (after two minutes): "In one more minute, Ella, it will be time to put the toys away." (*Small children have small memories and so may need more than one reminder.*)

Mother: "Now, let's see how good we can be at putting those toys away."

Mother helps Ella to put the toys away and all is well with the world! (*Positive expectation and appropriate involvement of Ella's mother.*)

OR

Although Mother gives the warning, Ella still protests about putting the toys away.

Ella: "I don't want dinner, I want to play."

Mother: "I know, you love playing with dolly." (*Ella's mother demonstrates empathy.*)

Ella: "She is my dolly."

Mother: "Of course she is and she is lucky to have

you. Ok, you put her over there in her bed for now or she can sit beside you and watch you eat your dinner." (*Ella is given a choice.*)

Ella: "She can watch me having dinner."

What has Ella possibly learned?

- She will be given time to finish doing what she is enjoying;
- Mother understands her love of her doll;
- There are choices that can be made to lessen the pain of separating from her dolly, if only temporarily;
- Mother is kind but she is also firm.

How might Ella feel?

- Happy;
- Loved.

The important principle to remember in relation to tantrums is:

PREVENTION IS BETTER THAN CURE.

There will be times when a parent fails to prevent the tantrum. Remember, it's not about getting it right all the time. The aim is to get it right 7 times out of 10.

If a tantrum is in progress:

- Stay calm;
- Ignore the tantrum and not the child. This means stay close to the child; keep your body language neutral;

avoid eye contact; and do not speak to the child. It can be a good idea to try some distraction when the child starts to calm down by looking out the window and commenting on something you see that you know the child would be interested in, e.g. "That cat seems to be looking for company out there." As soon as the child has stopped tantruming, give attention back;

- Do not refer to the tantrum that has just taken place. Instead, find something to praise the child for, e.g. "well done for calming down";
- If the child has thrown things around during the tantrum, it is important that the child cleans up, e.g. "We need to put these toys away nicely now and then we can..." Praise the child for compliance.

Key principle

Stay calm and kind.

> Remember, by staying *calm*, you are staying in control and your child sees this and it helps her to feel secure. If you lose your temper, you are no longer in control and this makes your child feel insecure and the misbehaviour escalates.

Meltdowns

Remember, a meltdown is caused by the intense fear or discomfort brought about in the child by some aspect of his environment at that moment.

Most adults can identify with the reaction brought about in them if someone scrapes a finger on the blackboard. We all have some sensory issues, i.e. an indescribable feeling of immense discomfort/pain when two objects make contact, e.g. a knife scratches along a plate, a stainless steel spoon makes contact with a stainless steel bowl, loud chewing noises, fingers turning pages.

This was brought into sharp focus for the author onc morning in the kitchen at the office where I worked. A colleague was using a stainless steel spoon to scrape some scraps of food out of the stainless steel sink. The noise made by this simple action caused me so much distress (I would liken it to a pain in my brain), that for some seconds I could not get the words out to ask her to stop. If I had been a child without the language to ask her to stop I would have hit and kicked her, such was the discomfort I was feeling and so great was my need for her to stop.

As with tantrums, PREVENTION IS BETTER THAN CURE. Children with atypical neural development, e.g. children with autism spectrum disorder (ASD), are more at risk of encountering elements in their environment that cause them to have meltdowns than are children whose neural system develops in the more usual way.

If loud noises or crowded places upset your child, there are a few principles to keep in mind:

- Does my child need to be in this environment in the first place – could I have gone shopping at a different time?
- Have you prepared your child for what he might encounter in this environment?
- Remember, your child is the EXPERT ON HIMSELF. Work with your child to discover what helps him in situations of sensory overload or extreme anxiety. For children who find loud noises painful, check if ear protectors are helpful. If your child finds unexpected change in the routine very anxiety provoking, ask him what will help him feel more secure. This is a process and it will take time to build up an understanding of what is upsetting the child in the first instance and what helps to offset the upset in the second place.

Changes in routine can also be upsetting for a child with ASD. If this is the case with your child, it is important that you prepare the child beforehand for the change. When doing this, use simple and concise language, e.g. "Dan, today we go to the shop first and then to Granny." Allow the child time to process this information and deal calmly with any protests.

It can be cruel to place a child in a situation that he finds difficult to tolerate. However, the solution *does not* lie in avoidance. Instead, it lies in understanding the difficulties and their causes and then working with the child to discover what makes these situations more tolerable for the child.

In doing this, you are building the invaluable skill of resilience.

Managing meltdowns

Nothing and nobody is perfect. Life is full of surprises: some pleasant; some very unpleasant. Even the most effective parent/carer may experience their child having a major meltdown. If/when this happens, the following tips are useful:

- If possible, remove the child from the stressful environment – noise, crowded space, etc.;
- If removal is neither necessary nor possible, stay close to the child. Take your lead from the child, go as near to the child as he will allow, do not overwhelm the child with your nearness if this upsets rather than calms him;
- Use soothing tones – "It's ok, it's ok, you are safe now, Mammy/Daddy is here." If your child reacts badly to your voice then stay quiet but near;
- If your child finds tight hugs soothing, give one; if your child prefers you at a distance, keep a distance but DO NOT LEAVE THE CHILD'S VICINITY;
- If there is a toy or object that your child finds soothing, gently offer it to the child;
- If there is a place your child finds soothing (a tight corner in the living room, under his blanket, etc.), allow the child to go there.

REMEMBER, YOUR CHILD IS NOT MISBEHAVING. HE IS IN A STATE OF IMMENSE FEAR OR DISCOMFORT AND YOUR ROLE IS TO HELP HIM TO FEEL SAFE AND COMFORTABLE AGAIN.

Key points

- Learn to discriminate between a TANTRUM and a MELTDOWN;
- Prevention is better than cure;
- Your child is his own expert – listen to his behaviour and words;
- Stay calm;
- Never give out to the child for the tantrum. Instead, focus on finding something in the child's behaviour to praise when he is calm again.

9

Biting

Biting is a misbehaviour that parents of toddlers and crèche workers sometimes find difficult to manage. Remember, all behaviour is a form of communication and so, in order to correct it, we need to understand what is being communicated. It is not uncommon to hear parents and crèche workers say of a child who bites:

> "He knows exactly what he is doing."
>
> "She does it to get attention."

The latter statement can be correct, the former only partially so, but it is upsetting to hear either or both being said in a hostile tone that attributes 'bad intent' to the child. If, however, parents and carers concern themselves with the communication behind the behaviour then we have EFFECTIVE parenting/caring in action.

Common reasons for biting

1. Attention

As discussed in the chapter on attention:

POSITIVE ATTENTION IS BEST, *NEGATIVE* ATTENTION IS SECOND BEST, *NO* ATTENTION CANNOT BE TOLERATED, AS IT MAY RESULT IN DEATH.

If a child is not getting sufficient positive attention, i.e. pleasant faces, smiles, hugs, having other needs met, etc., he will use negative attention in an endeavour to get these needs met. The innate drive for survival sets in and it drives the child's behaviour.

2. Communication

All behaviour is communicating something. Children may not have the verbal skills to make their needs/wants known, e.g. Billy, aged two, bites Sam, aged two, because Sam refuses to give Billy the train that Sam is playing with.

3. Sensory issues

A child can be over- or under-sensitive to touch. A child who has an oral under-sensitivity may use his mouth to get sensory input. A parent or carer can establish if this is the reason behind the biting behaviour by attending to the biting behaviour of the child, e.g. does the child bite objects more than might be expected of a teething child? Does he love using his toothbrush? Does he randomly bite another child/person?

This behaviour can be corrected by re-directing the child to suitable objects for biting on. Never tell a child: "No, you can't bite Mammy." Instead, redirect towards an acceptable biting object: "You need your chewy now."

Key principle

Tell the child what *to* do, not what *not* to do.
Wrong: "Don't bite."
Right: "Chewys are for biting on."

Managing biting behaviour or any misbehaviour involving another child or person

Give attention first to the victim. Example:

> Sasha, aged two-and-a-half, has bitten Ruby, aged two-and-a-half, while they were playing together at Sasha's house. Ruby screams and Sasha's mother immediately realises what has happened. She goes first to comfort Ruby.
>
> Mum: "Oh Ruby, you poor thing, that looks sore, I am sorry that happened to you."
>
> Most likely, now Sasha is standing by looking somewhat guilty. Mum turns to Sasha.
>
> Mum: "Sasha, Ruby is hurt. What can you do to make her feel better?"

Parents are often aghast at this recommendation and protest: "But Sasha has to learn she cannot bite Ruby or anyone else, she has to learn it is wrong." Their preferred response would be something like: "Sasha, that is so bold. You can't do that. Now you have to go and sit in the bold corner, but first you must tell Ruby you are sorry."

If the latter is your usual response, please take some time to reflect on the possible learnings for Sasha:

- She has learned that the behaviour is bold, and now she must sit in a place called the 'bold corner' so she must be bold. Her mother's tone and face tell her this is a very bad thing, so she must be bad. She has learned she must say 'sorry'. She is learning that there is a word – 'sorry'– which must be said sometimes.

How might Sasha feel?

- She is confused because she does not really know what she has done wrong. Ruby was playing with her favourite toy and she wanted it back. She feels sad and bad because her mother is cross with her. She feels alone, unhappy and confused about sitting in the 'bold corner'.

Also what might Ruby have learned?

- That being the offender is more important than being the victim, because the offender got more attention. Hurting someone results in getting into a lot of trouble.

How might Ruby feel?

- Sasha's mam is very cross with Sasha and that makes her afraid. She wants her own Mammy right now.

THE FORMER RESPONSE IS THE EFFECTIVE PARENTING RESPONSE FOR THE FOLLOWING REASON:

- The VICTIM gets the attention FIRST and is consoled

with empathy and kindness;
- The offending child's attention is brought to the fact that the other child is hurt. The offending child is then coached towards doing something to help her playmate feel better;
- This approach is cognizant of age and stage of both children. They are toddlers and, as such, have a very limited capacity for reasoning.

Finally, when both children are calm and ready for play again, it would be very important to do a little piece of coaching with both children that could take the following form:

> Mum: "Girls, what do we do when we want the toy the other person is playing with?"
>
> As these children are so young, they may not be able to give any answer to this question. If not, give them the answer.
>
> Mum: "We use our words and we ask for it. So, Sasha, you would say: 'Ruby, please may I have...'"

Again, remembering the tender age of both children, their language skills will be limited. However, they will still be able to make an attempt at saying "please...". That is all that is required.

Prevention is always better than cure. So be alert to opportunities for coaching the children in how to ask for what they want.

Key points

- Coach your child in the appropriate behaviour – "Say, 'please may I have...'";
- If your child has a tendency to bite, explore why this might be. The EarlyBird parenting programme[9] for the parents of children with autism spectrum disorder encourages parents to become DETECTIVES. This means reflecting on:
- what happened prior to the misbehaviour
- what happened during it
- what was the outcome;
- If one child bites the other, give attention first to the victim. Just enough to ensure the child is ok;
- Once the first child has received appropriate attention from you, turn your attention to the offending child and acknowledge firmly but kindly that her friend has been hurt;
- Invite the offending child to do something to make the victim feel better;
- Do not insist on the child saying sorry. Sorry is just a word, actions are what matter. Remember the model-

ling concept discussed in Part 1, Chapter 2. Children copy their parents' actions. If you say sorry when some action of yours has been harsh or hurtful, your child will learn to do the same. AND, BETTER STILL, WHEN THE CHILD SAYS SORRY, THE CHILD WILL BE SAYING WHAT HE FEELS!

10

Mealtimes and food issues

Many parents struggle with their children's issues around food and mealtimes. Remember, your child comes into the world equipped to seek out food and so the sucking instinct is there at birth. For the first four to six months, breast milk is all your child needs. If, for some reason, breast feeding is not an option for you, please do not worry. Infants need food, love and shelter. Once these are provided as needed your child will be just fine. It is often said that breastfed children are healthier. I breastfed my four children and witnessed the superior health of the same-aged, bottle-fed, neighbours' children!

When it is time to introduce solids to your infant, do so gradually and with the support and advice of the public health nurse, if you have a trusting relationship with her. If not, find someone whose knowledge in this area is trustworthy and seek support and advice as required.

Unfortunately, all too often, as your child grows from an infant to a toddler to a pre-schooler, problems with eating can develop.

If your child's difficulties are to do with sensory issues, or other health concerns,

SEEK SUPPORT FROM AN APPROPRIATE PROFESSIONAL.

Some children love and eat any food. However, it is unlikely that there is a child or adult who does not love some foods and feels disgusted by, or hates, others. Think back to your own childhood. Did you like all foods? Were you a fussy eater? How are you now? Do you eat some food now that you refused to eat as a child?

We who live in the 'First World' are very lucky to have many foods readily available. However, many parents must manage their family finances on small wages or benefits and have to budget carefully. When it comes to food, the good advice is to ensure a balanced healthy diet for your child. This need not cost a lot of money. I am often amazed that parents, who have little money to spare, give their child money to buy a lunch for school each day, rather than the cheaper alternative of a healthy packed lunch! Sugary foods, processed foods and foods high in fats, such as chips, should be treats in your house and not the mainstay diet.

If your child sometimes refuses to eat the food you offer, you have a child who is developing normally. If you give in to this refusal all the time you are most likely encouraging unhealthy eating habits in the child.

Below are four important principles in relation to food and food refusal:

1. Never fight with your child about food. If you do, you may be setting your child up for issues with food and control in her life. Instead, give a choice. The best choice is: 'eat or be hungry' . The old saying of 'hunger is good sauce' is, like a lot

of old sayings, true. Put the food aside and, when your child is hungry – and the child *will* be hungry – he will eat then;

2. Use the FIRST... THEN principle: "When you have eaten dinner, then you can have dessert/pudding/a biscuit." Treats are perfectly sound after a meal but the treat must not replace the meal!

> TREATS DIFFER FROM REWARDS IN THAT THEY ARE FOR SPECIAL OCCASIONS, E.G. DESSERT/PUDDING/BISCUIT AFTER THE MAIN MEAL, BIRTHDAY CAKE ON BIRTHDAYS, SWEETS AT PARTIES AND ON SUNDAYS, ETC.

3. Do not insist on your child eating everything on his plate. You know how hungry you are and not how hungry your child is. If your child eats a little dinner and half an hour later is looking for something else – but not as healthy as dinner – you know he is pushing boundaries (just as he is supposed to do). If there is no dinner left to offer, you can offer something else that is healthy. Do not get into the habit of giving sweet treats then as your child will develop an eating habit of a little healthy food and a lot of unhealthy food. Remember, you are setting up habits for life;

4. Some children, particularly those with autism spectrum disorder (ASD), can have a lot of difficulty with certain foods. The child may have a limited diet or may like the food cooked and served in a particular way. Do not view this as misbehaviour. If you are sure your child's dislike of certain foods, limited diet, etc., is caused by his condition, again do not fight with the child over this. You may need the advice of your GP

or a visit to a dietitian. However, best practice is to go with your child's preference but gradually encourage and reward attempts at extending the diet.

The following is another commonly reported mealtime situation.

Ineffective parenting response

> Molly, aged 4: "I don't want to eat that. It's yuck!"
>
> Mum: "Of course you want to eat it, Molly, it's good for you. You want to grow big and strong, don't you?"
>
> Molly: "Nooo... I want a biscuit."
>
> Mum: "If you don't eat up, you won't get any biscuit."
>
> Molly (starting to whinge): "I want a biscuit."
>
> Mum (getting cross): "Stop that whingeing and eat your dinner. You are not getting a biscuit until you eat your dinner."
>
> Molly (pushing the food around on her plate and continuing to whinge): "It's yuck."
>
> Mum: "Oh for God's sake, Molly, why do you have to be so difficult?! Just eat your dinner and stop whingeing."

Molly (eating a little dinner reluctantly): "I am full, now can I have a biscuit?"

Mum (really cross now): "You barely touched your dinner. No, you can't have a biscuit!"

Molly (starting to cry): "I hate dinner... I hate everyone!"

What is Molly learning here? What messages is she getting from her mother's response? Possibly that:

- Mealtime is a time of conflict;
- She makes her mother mad, but her mother is mean and wants her to eat yuck;
- She must eat her dinner before she gets a biscuit;
- Whingeing gets her lots of negative attention.

One thing is sure: neither Molly nor her mother are experiencing nice feelings right now.

Let's replay this scenario and, this time, we will use effective parenting skills.

Effective parenting response

Molly: "I don't want to eat that. It's yuck!"

Mum: "Molly, what's yuck about it?"

Molly: "I hate this dinner. Can I have toast instead?"

Mum: "This is what we are having now, Molly. Toast is for breakfast and maybe lunch. After you have eaten your dinner, you can have two biscuits. I have the ones you like – chocolate fingers."

(*Note: As having 'something sweet' after dinner is a healthy social behaviour and tradition – dinner first, then dessert – it is perfectly acceptable to use it as leverage here.*)

Molly: "Ok."

Molly eats a few spoonfuls and then says: "Finished."

Mum: "I think you might need to eat a little more, Molly, otherwise you will be hungry later and this is the last meal before bedtime. Let's see... four spoonfuls more?"

Molly: "Two spoonfuls."

Mum: "Let's say three, and we will high five on it." They high five and Molly eats the three spoonfuls.

Mum: "Good girl, Molly, for eating dinner. Now you can have the two biscuits." Mum gives Molly the biscuits and a hug.

Possible learnings for Molly:

- Mum is firm, kind and calm;
- Mum understands that Molly would prefer to eat her choice of food;
- Compromise is possible – agreeing things can be good;
- No snacking is allowed after dinner. Next meal is tomorrow's breakfast;
- Compliance gets positive attention, praise and the reward of a treat afterwards as this is dinner and a small treat is allowed after dinner.

Key points

- Never allow mealtimes to become a time of conflict;
- Give a choice – eat or not – however, next meal is at...;
- Take account of individual preferences – be kind and firm, not strict and harsh;
- Use FIRST... THEN. First we eat dinner, then we have desert; first we eat, then we play;
- Avoid using food as a reward. It is important for emotional and physical health that food does not become associated with making things feel better;
- Food treats are used sparingly. For instance, we have dessert after dinner. We have a birthday cake on our

birthday. We have an ice-cream at the beach. Giving a box of chocolates can be a nice way to say thanks to someone who did something really nice for the other person.

11

Bedtime

Bedtime is often a stressful time in the home. To resolve any situation that brings unwarranted stress it is useful to take some time and ask yourself a few questions. The answers to those questions should direct you towards the solution.

- What age is my child?
- What are my expectations? Are they reasonable?
- Does my child have any challenges or diagnosis that makes bedtime a difficult transition time?
- Has my child had any experience that could be causing a problem?
- Is this situation causing me extra stress that may be impacting my relationship with my child?

Let's take the last question first – STRESS. Every emotion we feel has a message and a reason. The feeling of stress is telling you that something needs to change, and if you keep doing what you have been doing it won't change and may get worse. Your next task is to look at what is really causing the stressed feeling. I say this because, in my own experience of parenting, and in my later experiences of working with parents, I often find that the stress is coming from the unfair expectation (question 2) we place on ourselves *or* from the expectation we think others have of us.

> REMEMBER, IF YOUR PARENTING STYLE IS PREDICATED ON BUILDING A POSITIVE RELATIONSHIP WITH YOUR CHILD, UNDERSTANDING AND RESPONDING TO YOUR CHILD'S 'NEEDS' RATHER THAN 'WANTS' AND SUPPORTING YOUR CHILD TOWARDS BECOMING A SELF-DISCIPLINED ADULT THROUGH APPROPRIATE RULES AND BOUNDARIES, YOU ARE BEING AN EFFECTIVE PARENT. BE PROUD OF YOURSELF.

Question 1, about your child's age, is important. Infants need a lot of sleep but often have a different sleeping pattern to ours. Instead of becoming stressed because your infant has not yet learned the rules of the world (!), try to adjust your own relationship with the rules of the world. Arrange your sleeping environment in such a way that you can get sleep when your infant does. As your child reaches toddlerhood and has developed some cognitive capacity, you can, if you wish, start to bring in some rules around bedtime. I say 'if you wish' because in my home, after failing miserably and becoming very stressed while following the expectations of others with my first child in relation to sleep, with my subsequent three children I did it my way! They fell asleep downstairs and were carried upstairs or they fell asleep with a parent beside them or in the parents' bed. I was less stressed and we were all happy, and they are no longer sleeping with me!

If your child has had a bad fright or experienced a

trauma – question 4 – you can expect some difficulties with sleep for a time. Research has shown that children exposed to frightening or traumatic situations report more frightening dreams or nightmares than children not so exposed or living in safer environments.[10] Some psychologists believe this to be an adaptive process and associated with recovery from the trauma.[11] However, the important message for parents here is that the impact of this on the child can be greatly lessened and eventually resolved with the following approach:

- Explain to your child that it is normal to have problems with sleep after an event such as the one that your child experienced. Use child-friendly language and do not overwhelm the child with too many words or too complicated an explanation. Say something like: "When someone has experienced something out of the ordinary like you did, sleep can be disturbed for a few nights";
- Inform the child that, after a while, he will return to his usual sleeping pattern;
- Ask her what would make her feel happier or less afraid at bedtime and during the night – night light, a soft toy, depending on your religious orientation an icon from your belief system, etc.;
- If she asks for you to sleep with her, it is best to suggest she sleep in her bed but you will be nearby if she needs you;
- If you are a parent who has no difficulty with your child coming into your bed at night, remind her that she can do this if she wakens during the night;
- If you are a parent who cannot sleep with your child

in the bed, remind him of where you will be during the night. Reassure him if he comes into your room during the night, and gently bring him back to bed and reassure him that morning will soon come and he will feel better. You may have to do this a few times during the night;

- A child's sleep disturbance can be – and almost always is – very exhausting for the parent. Do keep in mind that it is temporary and that the calmer and more reassuring you remain the shorter the duration of sleep disturbance for your child.

Children with a diagnosis of attention deficit hyperactivity disorder (ADHD) or autism spectrum disorder (ASD) often have difficulties with sleep – question 3. This can be very difficult for parents, and the parents often suffer sleep deprivation themselves. Unfortunately, there is no magic formula for dealing with this but the following tips should be helpful for all children:

- Having a bedtime routine is important for every child, and the predictability of it is especially helpful for children with ASD;
- Have a wind-down routine before bedtime. Television is turned off; if a bath helps, and if it is convenient for you to have this as part of the routine, supervise your child having one; pyjamas are put on, teeth are brushed; and finally it's story time. A short story is sufficient;
- Absolutely no TVs or screens in the bedroom. This is important – they are a bad, unhelpful habit. For some reason, it's not the same with aural stimulation. If your child

likes to listen to music or a story on a recorder, great;

- You cannot insist on your child going asleep. It is one of the truths of life that the harder one tries to go asleep the more one stays awake. Instead, you make a rule that once your child is in bed he stays in bed *but* you check on him regularly. Night time can be very scary for children. Everywhere is dark and quieter. So, regular check-ins reassure the child that he is not alone. This reduces stress in your child and, because she is relaxed, she is more likely to fall asleep;
- A night light in the room can be very helpful. As already said, children can struggle with the darkness of night time;
- If your child is struggling with staying in bed after bedtime, consider setting up a reward system. If the child manages to stay in bed until he falls asleep, the next morning he earns a sticker or a point. He also gets lots of praise and, at the end of the week, he can, if he wishes, trade in his sticker or points for a bigger reward. An ideal bigger reward could be staying up half an hour later at the weekend. The rationale here is to build a habit of staying in bed, and doing anything for long enough ensures it becomes a habit.

Of course, it is completely appropriate that children will test rules and boundaries. The parent's job is to know when to relax a rule and when to stay firm. The following scenario is one that a lot of parents describe. In the first instance, the parent responds ineffectively and then the scenario is re-worked using the skills learned in Part 1.

Jack, aged nine, has a bedtime of 8.30pm on school nights. He never likes going to bed and argues with his parents about it most nights. Tonight, he is watching TV when his Dad tells him it is time for bed.

Ineffective parenting response

Jack: "Just let me see the end of this programme."

Dad: "How much longer is left in the programme?"

Jack: "It will be over shortly."

Dad: "Jack, it is your bedtime and you are to go to bed right now."

Jack: "Ah no, Dad. Look, it's almost over..."

Dad (getting cross): "Let me see, there is another half an hour in that programme. Go to bed now, Jack."

Jack ignores his Dad and carries on watching the programme.

Dad (in a loud and cross voice): " Are you deaf? Go to bed NOW! I said NOW, Jack!"

Jack looks at his Dad and, seeing he is getting angry, slowly gets up. As his Dad advances angrily towards the television, he runs upstairs, saying loudly as he goes: "It's not fair, you are so mean..."

Mother, who has been in the kitchen, comes into the hallway as she hears the noise and says: "Please be quiet, ye will wake the baby. Jack, stop being bold and go to bed. There is no story for you tonight because you did not go to bed on time."

(*There could have been many variations of this scene: Dad and Jack might have argued back and forth for longer about going to bed; Jack might have shouted abuse at Dad; Dad might have given in and let Jack continue watching the programme; it might have escalated some more, with Dad shouting abuse and Jack in tears.*)

Possible learnings for Jack:

- What is Jack learning by Dad's response of getting angry? That getting angry is the way to solve problems? Aggression is a solution. Jack does not like it when his Dad gets angry and he obeys reluctantly but only because he is afraid of what might happen if he did not. He loses respect for his father;
- What is Jack learning by Dad giving in? That Dad is weak, does not like conflict and will give in if he protests enough. Although Jack gets to watch the end of the programme, it is not a happy win for him. He knows his Dad should have held firm. He loses respect for his Dad;
- If Dad engages in an argument with Jack, he is giving Jack lots of negative attention. A power struggle is play-

ing out and, in the end, Jack will have to go to bed. The atmosphere between Jack and Dad will be tense, with no good feelings for a time, at least.

Let's replay this scene and use tools that we have spoken of in Part 1.

Effective parenting response

Dad: "Jack, it's 8.20pm now and your bedtime is 8.30pm."

Jack: "Ah Dad, this is a great nature programme, can I watch until the end?"

Dad: "How much longer is left?"

Jack: "Not much..."

Dad: "Let's see... Oh, it doesn't end until 9pm. That's too late, Jack."

Jack: "Ah pleeease... it will be over real soon..."

Dad: "No, you have school tomorrow, Jack, and you need to go to bed now."

Jack: "Ah Dad, don't be so mean... I'll go to bed earlier tomorrow night."

Dad (in a firm but kind voice): "We will set the TV to record and you can watch the rest before bedtime tomorrow evening."

Jack (reluctantly): "Ok..."

Dad: "Good boy, Jack. I'll be up to say goodnight in about 10 minutes when you have brushed your teeth and are in bed."

Using effective parenting skills:

- Dad prepared Jack for the ending of TV time by giving a 10-minute warning. Children love surprises, but only if they are pleasant ones;
- Dad checked the time at which the programme would end and, when he discovered it was going to end half an hour after Jack's bedtime, he remained firm but kind – he suggested taping the rest of the programme and Jack watching it during TV time tomorrow, if he chooses – regarding the rules;
- He praises Jack's compliance;
- He reminds Jack he will be up to say goodnight (and maybe read a story if Jack would like one) when Jack is in bed;
- Jack may not be happy that he has to go to bed but his respect for Dad grows as Dad has stayed calm and respectful. Very importantly, Dad has modelled for Jack how to behave in challenging situations.

'Mommy, I want a drink of water'

The above is the title of a song from my childhood about a child who tries in vain to re-engage his mother's attention with calls and stories after going to bed. This scenario and the child who keeps coming downstairs can be stressful for the parent who is looking forward to some well-earned rest and relaxation. It is not uncommon for parents to respond calmly at first but eventually to give in to annoyance and frustration and get cross with the child. Later, when the child has eventually settled to sleep, the parent often feels guilty and uneasy about the negative attention that the child's behaviour resulted in.

Setting up a reward system is the ideal way of dealing with this situation.

> PLEASE KEEP IN MIND THE FOLLOWING TRUISM: A CHILD WILL WORK A LOT HARDER TO EARN A REWARD – A POSITIVE CONSEQUENCE – THAN HE WILL TO AVOID A NEGATIVE CONSEQUENCE – SUCH AS TAKING THINGS AWAY.

Setting up the reward system

1. Sit with the child at a time when both of you are calm and relaxed.
2. Start with praise, e.g. "Oisin, I really appreciate that you are doing such a good job of being ready for school on time, thank you for that."
3. Then state the behaviour you want to change. "You

know how you are in and out of bed after going upstairs at night and eventually I get mad and shout at you? Neither of us likes that. Well, I have an idea of how to change that."

4. Explain how the system will work, e.g. "Oisin, when you are in bed and we have said goodnight I expect you to stay in bed until you fall asleep. I know this can be difficult for you. So you staying in bed and not calling me or leaving the bed will earn you a point or sticker. When you have *x* number of points/stickers earned you can trade them in for..." Linking the concrete reward to the behaviour you want to reinforce can be very successful. "So, when you have 5 points – that is when you have stayed in bed and did not call me back to the room for five nights – you can trade in your points and stay up half an hour later than your usual bedtime." However, the reward must be reinforcing for the child. The point/sticker in the first place is a reward and the added reward of accumulating the points/stickers and the child earning something he would like is an extra reinforcement. For children under the age of six, a sticker each morning may be sufficient. For older children, agreeing what that can be traded in for is important. For an older child who likes to earn money, 20 cent for staying in bed becomes 1 euro after five nights and could be used to buy something the child likes, but would not ordinarily get. Alternatively, the child can save each 20 cent for something more expensive.

5. If the child does not succeed in staying in bed when first tried, calmly remind the child of the reward that can be earned and that tomorrow is another night and you trust he will succeed then. If, on the second night, there is no success, you need to review the strategy. If he is leaving the bed sev-

eral times before sleep, maybe expecting him to change this immediately is too great an initial expectation. Perhaps you need to agree that he can leave the bed just once or that he stays in bed for 10 minutes and then you will visit him, give lots of praise and next you will visit in 15 minutes, etc. An anxious child may need the reassurance of your presence after an interval to relax enough to sleep. THE IMPORTANT THING IS THAT THE REWARD IS MOTIVATING, IT CAN BE ACHIEVED, HE GETS REWARDED FOR SUCCESS AND GETS EMPATHY AND HOPE FOR FUTURE SUCCESS IF HE DOES NOT ACHIEVE SUCCESS AT FIRST.

(Incredible Years parenting programme[3] informed the strategies.)

> PRACTISE AND MAKE 'FIRM *AND* KIND' YOUR PERFECT RESPONSE FOR EVERY CONTENTIOUS ISSUE.

KEY POINTS

- Have a bedtime routine that is positive and relaxing;
- From early in your child's life, sing a lullaby and later read a bedtime story to/with your child;
- You cannot command or demand sleep – you can have a rule of staying in bed;

- Use a reward system to encourage good bedtime habits, i.e. staying in bed;
- Have a rule which states that screens of any type can only be used downstairs – no TVs or phones in the bedroom.

12

Bullying

Bullying is defined by the Department of Education and Skills guidelines as unwanted negative behaviour, verbal, psychological or physical, conducted by an individual or group against another person (or persons) and which is repeated over time.[12]

It is important to note the word, *repeated.* A one-off incident of something unpleasant suffered by your child at the hands of another child does not constitute 'bullying'. It has to be repeated for it to warrant the definition of bullying.

As with other incidents of misbehaviour there is always learning involved. A key concept in 'effective parenting' is that something 'hurtful' and 'harmful' can become an opportunity to promote and build RESILIENCE in the child.

Another key concept in a problem situation is that the parent does not step in to solve the problem but rather *supports* the child in solving *his* problem. When this is done effectively you are giving your child important life skills.

Please also keep in mind that calling a child a 'bully' is unhelpful. A child's behaviour may constitute 'bullying' in one situation and in another situation the same child may be the *victim* of bullying behaviour. This is true of all of us. We all have within us the potential to be the bullied and to do the bullying.

The concept of MODELLING was discussed in Chapter 2. If a child comes from a home where a parent or parents overuse their power in order to control the children this is 'bullying behaviour'. It should be no surprise then, since children learn more powerfully from what we do rather than what we say, that this child is at risk of abusing his power over a child if he senses a potential weakness in the other child.

To be the victim of bullying brings a lot of negative feelings but chief among them is a feeling of *powerlessness.*

Ineffective parenting response

> Marcus is nine years old and confides in his mother that another boy, Glenn, is bullying him at school. The bullying involves calling Marcus names and encouraging other boys in the classroom not to play with him. Marcus is very upset.
>
> Mother: "The little brat. How dare he treat you like that. You tell him he is not to do that and that if this continues he will have to answer to me."
>
> Marcus (crying): "He will just laugh at me, and so will the others."
>
> Mother (angry and concerned): "He is a brat and has no right to treat you like that. I will go and talk to the teacher about this. I will ring his mother and tell her what he is doing."

Marcus (fearfully): "Please don't do that. It will only make it worse."

Mother: "Marcus, I have to tell teacher and his mother. He can't continue to do this to you. It won't get worse, I promise you."

Marcus is not happy about this, but seems to reluctantly agree.

Parents often respond in a similar fashion to the mother above. It is understandable that the parent would respond thus. It is a very distressing thing for a parent to see his child emotionally upset. It is even more upsetting to learn that this upset is being caused by another child's bullying behaviour. The parent's instinct is to fix this immediately. However, this is not the most effective approach, as we will see when we look at what Marcus has learned from his mother's response:

- His mother cares very much for him and it upsets her greatly to see him upset;
- He is not sure he can trust her not to make the situation worse;
- He feels he has no power and can't solve this himself.

Effective parenting response

Mother: "Marcus, I am very sorry to hear that. It must be very upsetting for you?" (*Empathy.*)

Marcus (crying): "Yeah..."

Mother puts her arms around Marcus, holds him gently and allows his tears to flow. (*Supportive and consoling.*)

Marcus: "I hate Glenn, he is so mean... and horrible..."

Mother: "I can understand you feeling like that, Marcus. It is horrible when somebody treats us so badly. Do you want to tell me what names he calls you?" (*Empathic response and an open question. Also note the judgement of the behaviour and not the person.*)

Marcus (crying again): "No, they are too horrible..."

Mother (hugging Marcus): "You poor thing, this is really horrible for you. The good news, though, is we can make this better." (*Empathic and respectful acceptance of Marcus's reluctance to reveal the names. Clear statement that this will get better.*)

Marcus: "How? Nothing works... he is just a bully."

Mother: "Yes, he is behaving very badly. What do you do when he calls you those names?" (*Again, the behaviour and not the person is judged. Enquire as to how Marcus has tried to solve this himself.*)

Marcus: "I have tried telling him to shut up, but he just gets worse and then he gets the other boys to join in and call me even worse names."

Mother: "That is really horrible. I am very glad you are telling me this. You are very brave to have tried to fix this by telling him to stop. Does teacher know this is happening?" (*Empathy, praise and relevant question regarding the teacher.*)

Marcus: "I don't know, but she never does anything to him anyway. He is often bold in class and gets away with it."

Mother: "Together, we will work out a way to stop this, Marcus. You are describing bullying behaviour and I am so glad you told me about it, because it is too serious for you to sort on your own. I am going to be with you every step of the way until this is stopped, and it will stop." (*Clear communication about seriousness of behaviour, that Marcus cannot sort this on his own but it can be sorted.*)

Marcus: "Thanks, Mam."

Mother: "Let's get started on a plan. Because this is so serious and is happening in school, teacher and the principal need to be informed about it." (*Clearly informing Marcus about what needs to happen.*)

Marcus: "Oh no, please don't do that. That will make it worse and I will be called a 'baby'."

Mother: "Yes, I can see how this is a worry for you.

How about I ring and make an appointment with your teacher and the principal for after school tomorrow? I can tell them it is very important and we need to meet as soon as possible." (*More empathy and at the same time staying on message that the school has to know.*)

Marcus: "Oh, but you will be seen at the school and I will get called a 'baby'."

Mother: "Ok. How about I ring the principal in the morning and tell her it is very important that I meet her but it is also very important that I am not seen at the school. We can then work out how that can be done. You are suffering, Marcus, and we are not going to allow that to continue. It is my responsibility to support you in stopping this. It is the school's responsibility to ensure that school is a happy place for you and all the children who attend there. They also have a responsibility towards the boy who is bullying you. He needs help to behave respectfully towards others. I would be surprised if you were the only one he is behaving like this towards." (*Taking into account Marcus's fears, his mother has a solution to offer.*)

Marcus: "He is mean and so are his friends, but he is the worst."

Mother: "You were very brave to tell him to stop. Is there anything else you could do?" (*Praise and exploration of what Marcus can do.*)

Marcus: "I don't think so."

Mother: "What do you usually do when you are being called those names?"

Marcus: "I feel like crying and try not to, because then it would get worse but sometimes they notice that and they call me a 'cry baby'."

Mother: "You feel very alone when in these situations. Can you think of anything different that you could do? People who engage in this type of behaviour can be quite cowardly. If they were brave like you they would not need to make others feel sad." (*Empathy and context as to why a person might behave like this.*)

Marcus: "I could walk away and play with someone else, but the awful thing is everyone is afraid of him and if they play with me then he starts on them, too."

Mother: "Walking away is a great idea, Marcus. Bad behaviour needs an audience and a response that the badly behaving person likes. This is a serious situation. Can you trust me to set up that appointment with the principal, no later than tomorrow, because this needs to be stopped immediately?" (*Praise again and respect for Marcus's feelings.*)

Marcus: "Ok."

Mother: "I will tell you exactly what happens at that meeting. You can come with me if you like?"

Marcus: "No, just tell me."

Mother: "I will, Marcus, and we will look again at what you can do to stand up to that behaviour. I know that is not easy but you have already been very wise and brave in trying to deal with it yourself and now in telling me. Be very proud of yourself. I have 20 minutes now before I need to start preparing dinner. How about a game of..."

Using effective parenting skills throughout, Mother has brought Marcus to a position where he is trusting of her not to make things worse. She is rightly taking responsibility for informing the school and working with them towards a solution as this is a serious situation where Marcus is being hurt emotionally. She is also continuing to request Marcus's opinions and making it clear to him that he has good ideas that are also essential in solving this problem. This is RESILIENCE BUILDING.

Key points

- The steps outlined in Chapter 6 are essential to this process;
- Bullying is an abuse of power and, as such, the child feels POWERLESS. A key element of the solution is to EMPOWER the child;
- Empathy is used at every stage in the process;
- The child's worries must be listened to as the parent works *with* the child to advance a solution in which the child can trust that the parent will not make the situation worse;
- As bullying always involves HURT, either emotional or physical, the parent must involve herself in the solution. This is too big for the child to handle alone;
- Remember, by working with your child towards an appropriate solution you are building resilience in the child;
- If your child has a tendency to be a victim of bullying or to be the perpetrator in bullying situations, it would be important that you seek help from a professional to explore this further.

13

Children fighting and time out

Parents often express exasperation at the rivalry or fighting that goes on between their children. If you have children who get on perfectly well all of the time, consider your family unique! It is absolutely normal that children disagree, argue and sometimes fight. The good news is that you can influence this behaviour for the better. You can even use these situations to build resilience in your child, which will benefit your child throughout his life. Let's consider the following common scenario.

Ineffective parenting response

> Chloe, aged seven, and her brother Jamie, aged nine, are playing and watching TV in the sitting room while Dad is doing some work on his computer in the kitchen. He hears shouting in the other room and then Chloe runs into the kitchen crying.
>
> Chloe: "Jamie hit me..."

Dad (ignoring Chloe, gets up from his computer with an angry look on his face and goes into the sitting room): "Jamie, what did you hit your sister for?"

Jamie: "She is just a cry baby, I did not hit her." He continues watching TV.

Chloe (who has followed Dad into the sitting room): "You did, you did."

Jamie: "I did not, you are just a liar."

Dad: "Would the two of you just be quiet. Jamie, did you hit your sister?"

Jamie and Chloe together: "I did not"... "You did, you did"... and now Chloe hits Jamie.

Dad: "Oh for goodness sake, you are one as bad as the other. Turn off that TV and go out to play. I have work to do and I can't do it with the two of you fighting."

Jamie: "Ah no, I was watching this programme and it's great."

Chloe: "He is just a big bully and..."

There could have been many variations to the dialogue and actions of Dad and the two children. The core issue is that Dad gets into the argument. Chloe does to Jamie what he did to her. Dad is frustrated and the situation does not resolve in any satisfactory way for any of the family members.

What is the possible learning for the children?

- That the victim (Chloe, who complained in the first instance that she had been hit) is ignored while attention is directed to the accused/offender (Jamie, who is the accused) – bad behaviour gets attention quicker than good behaviour. PLEASE NOTE THAT THE OUTCOME OF DAD IGNORING CHLOE AND GIVING ATTENTION TO JAMIE RESULTED IN CHLOE HITTING JAMIE AND NOW BOTH ARE GETTING DAD'S ATTENTION!;
- Dad is not able to resolve the situation to anyone's satisfaction. Instead of less hitting there is more hitting, as Chloe now hits Jamie;
- Arguments are tried as a solution to conflict. When this inevitably fails, Dad gives up;
- The children lose some respect for Dad.

Now let's replay this scenario using effective parenting skills.

Effective parenting response

Chloe: "Jamie hit me."

Dad (putting his arm around Chloe if she allows this): "Oh Chloe, Are you ok? What happened?"

Chloe: "We were watching TV and Jamie wanted to

watch his programme and I wanted to watch mine."

Dad: "A dilemma, I see. And how did you try to change Jamie's mind about watching his programme?"

Chloe: "I asked him but he always says no and it's not fair."

Dad: "Yeah, and when he would not agree, you maybe tried to change channel?"

Chloe: "But how else can I watch my programme? He always gets his way."

Dad: "And then he hit you. Well, it is not ok that he hit you. Let's go now and hear what Jamie has to say."

Dad: "Jamie, pause that programme please."

Jamie: "Ah, but it's just at the good part."

Dad: "You can pause it or turn it off." Jamie hesitates. "Or I can do it for you?"

Jamie (reluctantly pausing the programme): "She tried to change the channel and I was watching first."

Dad: "Ok Jamie, Chloe has already told me that. The first thing here is that hitting is never a solution to a problem. Jamie, you need to take a time out (explained below) and think of appropriate and safe ways of responding in future when something like this happens. Think of how to resolve a dilemma like this in a way that no one gets hurt and the situation gets resolved. Stay here in the sitting room as you do this. Chloe, I'd like you to also think of how you can resolve the problem of two people wanting to watch different programmes at the same time. When Jamie's time out is finished we will sit down and discuss the ideas that both of you have."

What have both children possibly learned?

- The victim gets the attention first and is empathised/sympathised with;
- Everyone's voice is heard and respectfully listened to;
- Dad is firm but kind. He gives choices – pause or turn off the TV, the child does it or Dad does it;
- Every problem has a satisfactory solution.

Time out

Time out is a wonderful strategy to help children and parents manage emotions and behaviours. However, it is a very misunderstood and misused concept and strategy. The Incredible Years parenting programme has informed my thinking on this very useful concept and strategy.

- As time out necessitates an ability to comprehend and reason on the part of the child, it is not suitable for children under the age of three;

- Time out is *time out to calm down*. Note the very important 'to calm down';
- It is only used when the child has engaged in specific behaviour. For instance, if one child hits another, as instanced above, or if a child is in a heightened emotional state and spending time using calming strategies would be useful;
- The rationale for time out and the steps involved have to be explained to the child at a time when there is a nice, calm atmosphere between the parent and child. Unfortunately, a lot of parents send children angrily to time out at a time when both are emotionally aroused and the child has never been told what time out is about or how to do it!;
- The child stays in time out only for as long as it takes the child to calm down. If a child is shouting and arguing or angrily crying, time out does not end until about two minutes after the child has calmed down;
- Time out is ended by the parent saying something like: "Well done, Jamie, for calming down. Please help me with... or... if you like you can go out to play now... or... NOTE THE PARENT DOES NOT REFER TO THE INCIDENT THAT RESULTED IN A TIME OUT IN THE FIRST PLACE;
- Time out can be seen as *time out from good attention*. This means that the parent does not engage with the child while he is on time out. As you will see below, the child has the very important job of calming down when in time out. A lot of parents make the mistake of giving out to, and about, the child when in time out. This means that the child is getting negative attention,

which will damage the relationship between parent and child, as well as discouraging the child in his attempts to do the right thing.

In time out the child:

- Is *actively involved* in calming-down strategies. It is very important that you have discussed this with your child. There are common strategies that work for most of us, i.e. breathing slowly and concentrating on our breath. Ask your child what else might be helpful for her. For instance, some children/adults may find counting to 20 or/and backwards from 20 helps to calm down;
- The child *thinks* of how to manage a situation such as the one that resulted in a time out, if/when it occurs in the future. So, Jamie may decide that next time, if Chloe interrupts his TV programme, he will pause the TV and inform her how long his programme is going to take. Or he may decide they need to agree who watches TV at what time. Or... or... or...;
- The child leaves time out when the parent says something like: "Well done, Jamie, you are nice and calm now, you can go back to playing with Luke";
- Time out started with the child being timed out of the parent's good attention. It ends with the child being timed back in. This is done by the parent giving the child some positive attention. For instance, if Jamie is now playing nicely with Luke, his parent says something like: "Great to see you two having fun again."

Key points

- Always remember to give attention to the behaviour you want to see more of – notice the children when they *are* behaving;
- If you are lucky enough to see a situation that may develop into a row, intervene with a reminder of the behaviour you wish to see, e.g. "Children, remember, playing nicely is a rule of this house" or "sharing TV time is important, do we need to discuss this?";
- Use positive (rewards) rather than negative (sanctions) consequences to encourage the appropriate behaviour. For instance, if your child has difficulty sharing toys, etc, set up a system that each time you witness the child sharing he earns a sticker (if under five) or a point (if older) that can be traded in for a bigger reward such as extra TV time when he has *x* number of stickers/points earned;
- Time out can be a wonderful strategy for helping a child to gain control of negative emotions that lead to dangerous misbehaviour;
- Never issue a time out command unless your child understands exactly what it means;
- Model taking time out yourself when you are feeling stressed or overwhelmed;

- After the child has completed the time out, remember to be alert for the opportunity to comment positively or praise something your child is engaged in.

14

Refusing to do

Psychiatrists sometimes diagnose a child as having oppositional defiant disorder (ODD). The *Diagnostic and Statistical Manual of Mental Disorders* (DSM–5, 2013)[13] provides this diagnosis if certain conditions are met. As with many diagnoses of a mental rather than a physical nature, it is based on self and/or other reports.

In the case of children, it is the parents who are the main information providers. It is the nature of children to test boundaries and this can, at times, lead to opposition and defiant-type behaviour. It is also true that some children are more stubborn than others. However, I *loathe* the diagnosis of ODD because:

- It does not inform as to why the child is refusing to comply;
- It places blame on the child;
- It offers no positive alternative;
- We would/should all be oppositional and defiant if we perceived ourselves as being unfairly asked to comply.

In my experience, if the adults – parents, teachers, etc. – responsible for the child's development, change their responses to the child's defiant behaviour, it inevitably brings about a positive change.

As stated in Chapter 5, if there was no consequence for breaking a law, such as speeding on the road, most of us would speed at least some of the time. If you want your child to obey reasonable rules, you must firstly ask politely and clearly. Ensuring the child hears and understands the request is vital. Then you must give the child time to comply. Obviously, if the child is engaged in dangerous behaviour such as hitting another child, that behaviour must stop immediately. Sometimes you may have to separate the children, by placing your body between theirs. However, if the child's refusal is in relation to a behaviour that does not put anyone's safety at risk, wait a few seconds after issuing the command. If the child is ignoring you or expressing his refusal verbally, remind the child of the choice he has. For instance: "Zac, please put your bag under the stairs and then you can go and play with your friends." The choice for Zac is clear: if he refuses to put his bag under the stairs he does not go to play with his friends.

Maybe Zac does not want to play with his friends, or doesn't care about playing with his friends. In that case, he may be tardy about complying with your request. However, a child's life involves far more play or fun time than an adult's life. So if Zac is refusing to comply with your request or ignoring your command it is the essence of EFFECTIVE PARENTING to ensure that Zac does not get to do the fun thing he has planned until he has completed the task. Perhaps he is going to watch TV, play a computer game, etc.

Parents who have been introduced to the FIRST... THEN or WHEN... THEN rule are fulsome in their praise of how effective it is. The following is a common enough example given by parents. As is usual in Part 2, the scene is played with an ineffective response often used by parents and then replayed using EFFECTIVE PARENTING SKILLS.

> Sasha, aged 11, pleaded with his parents for a dog as his birthday present. His parents consented after Sasha agreed that he would pick up the poop from the garden each day after school. The dog – Lulu – has now been living with the family for three weeks.

Ineffective parenting response

> Dad: "Sasha, please pick up the poop in the garden!"
>
> Sasha: "No, it's yuck! You do it."
>
> Dad: "Sasha, you got the dog because you agreed that you would clean the garden after him. Now do it!"
>
> Sasha: "In a minute..."
>
> Dad: "You had better do it in a minute!"
>
> Dad goes back to doing whatever he has been doing in the kitchen and forgets about Sasha for about 15 minutes.
>
> He remembers and shouts: "Sasha, have you cleaned the garden?"

Sasha, who is playing with his phone in his bedroom, ignores his Dad.

Dad is now angry and shouts up the stairs: "Sasha, go out to the garden immediately and clean up after that dog!"

Sasha: "I don't want to clean up after her. Anyway, she is not my dog. She is the family dog."

Dad is angrier now and stomps his way upstairs.

Dad: "Get off that phone immediately and do as you are told. Otherwise that Lulu is going."

Sasha: "Let her go then. I hate cleaning up after her. Someone else can do it for a change."

Dad: "Oh, for God's sake. I knew this would happen. Gimme that phone and go and do what you are told."

As Sasha hesitates some more, Dad grabs the phone from him.

Sasha is not happy and mutters under his breath...

Dad: "What did you say? Show your father some respect. I never spoke to my father like that."

Sasha reluctantly goes to the garden and does a poor

> job of cleaning up the poop. Dad stands angrily over him and gives out to him for his poor attempt. However, Dad is fed up of the confrontation now and goes back indoors, telling Sasha he will get his phone back tomorrow. Later, Dad relents and gives Sasha his phone back.

This scene could have played out in any manner of ways. Dad might have adopted a passive parenting approach (passive parenting involves the parent abdicating responsibility for ensuring that household rules are complied with), and accepted Sasha's refusal to clean the garden and cleaned it up himself. Sasha might have called his mother to intervene or might have continued to object. The disagreement could have continued into an unpleasant argument between father and son.

Regardless of what ensued after Sasha's initial refusal to clean up, there is learning involved for Sasha and it may include:

- Getting angry gets things done;
- Dad is not prepared to listen to the reasons for Sasha's reluctance to comply;
- Refusal to comply works – this is the learning if Dad accepts Sasha's refusal and does the task himself.

Sasha's respect for Dad will suffer in any of the above scenarios and the relationship will be negatively impacted. If the interactions between Dad and Sasha are usually more positive than negative, this will be a temporary glitch.

Effective parenting response

Dad: "Sasha, please pick up the poop in the garden!"

Sasha: "No, it's yuck! You do it."

Dad: "Yes, I know, it's not the most pleasant of tasks. When it's done you can go out to play or have your screen time."

Sasha: "Please, Dad, will you do it, just for today? I really hate doing it."

Dad: "We had a conversation about this, Sasha, before you got Lulu, and you agreed to clean her poop from the garden. If I am remembering correctly, you said you would walk her every day also. But your mother and I thought that might not work out, so we agreed on this task instead."

Sasha: "I like having her, I really do, but cleaning up the poop... and anyway, I am not the only one that gets fun out of her."

Dad: "That is true, Sasha. Here's the deal, you clean up the poop for the rest of the week. Then on Saturday we will have a family chat about it and share out the 'dog minding' duties with everyone who enjoys Lulu. That is, if you are prepared to share her with the rest of the family?"

Sasha: “If it means cleaning less poop, I am.”

Dad: “Thanks Sasha. Go and clean the poop now and then you can have fun.”

What has Sasha leaned?

- Rules are to be complied with *but* Dad is willing to listen to Sasha’s problem with a rule. This is a really important point. In all conflict situations, aim for a ‘firm but kind’ approach. The opposite is ‘strict and harsh’. Neither approach is about ‘giving in’. However, the former approach is about listening and respect, the latter is dogmatic and lacks respect for the child’s point of view. The former builds relationships, the latter fractures relationships;
- Difficulties and differences of opinion can be resolved in a calm manner;
- Work/tasks come first and then fun/leisure;
- Dad has demonstrated respect for Sasha by listening to him. However, the rule is still in place and Sasha has to comply with it until Saturday at least. Sasha respects Dad for being firm but fair. Dad’s response to Sasha’s objection was at all times conducted in a firm but kind tone and thus their relationship will be enhanced.

Key points

- Have rules and boundaries that are clearly and positively stated and understood by the children;
- Some rules also apply to you, e.g. respectful language;
- Use the FIRST... THEN or WHEN... THEN rule where necessary in order to ensure compliance;
- FIRM BUT KIND is your mantra.

15

Anxiety

The increase in the numbers of children getting a diagnosis of anxiety in Ireland was the subject of a May 2018 article in *The Irish Times*[14]. One week later, a similar article appeared in *The Sunday Times Magazine*[15], which reported an alarming increase in the number of children suffering similar symptoms in the UK. However, it is my experience that anxiety, as a condition, is, with the right mix of education and therapy, very manageable.

Anxiousness itself can be described as an emotion and, like all emotions, it is neither good nor bad. However, the feeling that accompanies an emotion is either pleasant or unpleasant. The condition, anxiety, embodies more than one emotion. Fear, confusion, terror, tension and unease are some of the emotions that can be experienced when one is anxious. It is often difficult for an adult to describe the feelings he or she is having when in a state of great anxiety or panic. Therefore, it will be even more difficult for a child to describe or name the emotions felt at this time. Emotions are primarily messengers and it is important that attention is paid to the message. However, because the condition known as anxiety arises internally in the individual and with no obvious external cause, understanding the message can be difficult, if not, at times, impossible.

So far, the term 'condition' has been used in relation to anxiety. This is to differentiate between the *condition* anxiety and *normal* anxiety. We can all be in an anxious state from time to time. It is a normal and very important part of being human. However, anxiety, like other things in life, exists on a spectrum. Too little anxiety and we may be too slow to do important things, too much and we may be impeded in doing important things.

The 'quick' and the 'dead', as explained by Joseph Le Doux in his excellent book, *The Emotional Brain*[16], can be a good way of understanding the importance of appropriate anxiety. Imagine you are about to cross the road, you catch a glimpse of car driving towards you, you jump out of the way and are safe – 'the quick'. Or the same scenario – a car driving towards you and you hesitate – 'the dead'.

This is not a therapy book, so it is not necessary to go into the symptoms, causes and treatments of anxiety in detail. However, it is important that, as a parent, you have a general understanding of anxiety in order to be able to support your child in managing the condition, should it arise.

If your child is experiencing anxiety that is impacting negatively on her everyday life, it is important to address this. In the first instance, ask yourself the following questions:

- Do you or anyone else in the family or extended family suffer from anxiety? Or has anyone suffered in the past?
- If you suffer from anxiety, how do you manage it? Does it work for you?

- If you suffered in the past, what helped? What did not help?
- How do you respond when your child says he is anxious or afraid?
- How do you respond when your child refuses to go somewhere or to do something because of anxiety?
- Is your child's anxiety in relation to specific situations? For instance, school, going somewhere without you, going to unfamiliar places,etc.

Your answers to the questions above will be very informative and important in understanding why your child may be anxious in the first place and, secondly, whether your response is helping your child learn essential life skills for managing fearful situations or maintaining your child's belief that he must avoid fearful situations.

1. An anxious temperament is often an inherited trait. In other words, someone else in the family or extended family has struggled, or is struggling, with anxiety.

2. If you suffer or struggle with anxiety it is essential that you examine how you manage it. If your management strategy is working for you, and does not involve avoiding the situations that make you anxious or an over-reliance on medication, then perhaps you should share this with your child. If your management involves avoidance, your child is most likely aware of this and, remembering the modelling concept, is copying what you are doing by avoidance also.

3. If your experience of troublesome anxiety is a memory, why do you think this is? Is it because of effective management skills? Did it just go away? Was it connected to a specific time

or event in your life? What has this taught you about how to manage anxiety? How about sharing this in age-friendly language with your child?

4. Your response to your child's anxiety is of vital importance, and effective parenting strategies are used in the example below. If your response involves minimising your child's fears, i.e. "you'll be grand", you need to change it to an empathic response, i.e. "I know that makes you feel uncomfortable"; "those feelings are not nice"; "I am sorry that you are feeling like that". After first showing empathy towards your child, it is important to then give a hopeful message, i.e. "It is quite common for children and adults to sometimes feel as you do now. The good news is it will get better."

5. If your response is to 'give in' or 'give out', you need to change it. Parents sometimes describe themselves as being 'soft' and 'giving in' because watching their child suffer is too difficult. These parents often mistakenly equate 'soft' and 'kind' as the same thing. They are not. Soft is about saving oneself from uncomfortable feelings or thoughts. Kind is about putting your child's feelings ahead of your own. A kind parent endures discomfort in order to support his child in finding solutions to problems.

6. If your child's anxiety is in relation to a specific situation it is important to explore what it is about the situation that is making the child fearful. Also, it is very important to explore if it is the situation that the child is going into or the situation the child is leaving behind which is causing the fear. For instance, it is not unusual in a 'school refusal' situation to find that it is not a fear of school or anything connected with school that is causing the child distress. Instead, the child is

afraid of what may happen to you while she is away. Have you had an unplanned hospital admission? Is your home an unsafe place? Is there anything else that your child could be worried about happening while he is at school?

Coaching and supporting your child to manage anxiety

If anxiety is causing your child problems, the problem-solving chapter (Chapter 6) of Part 1 will provide you with all the tools you need to help.

Sometimes, when a child is experiencing significant anxiety, he or she may refuse to go to school. In the following scenario, Ayesha, aged 11, is telling her mother that she does not want to go to school tomorrow. Ayesha's mother is aware that, for the past few months, Ayesha has been anxious about lots of things. She was always a nervous child but seems to have gotten more nervous lately. She is not as keen to go to friends' parties and refused an offer to stay over at a friend's house recently.

> Ayesha: "Mammy, please do not make me go to school tomorrow!"
>
> Mother: "But you have to go to school, Ayesha. You love school."
>
> Ayesha (tearfully): "I don't. I hate it and I am not going!"

> Mother: "This is not like you, Ayesha. What is the matter?"
>
> Ayesha: "Nothing. I just don't want to go to school, I hate it."
>
> Mother: "You really are upset, Ayesha. I am sorry to hear you no longer like school. I wonder why that is?"
>
> Ayesha: "I don't know..."
>
> Mother: "I have noticed that you are reluctant to go places lately. For instance, you did not go to Fatima's sleepover last week..."
>
> Ayesha: "I didn't want to go and I don't want to go to school."

Of note here, this conversation could take a number of directions. Ayesha may tell her mother she is afraid and does not know why. She may describe a 'hot tummy' or she may refuse to talk about it any longer. If she refuses to talk about it anymore it is better not to push it right now. STAYING HOME FROM SCHOOL IS NEVER A SOLUTION FOR ANXIETY, and therefore her mother must stay firm but kind. It is important to say something like: "I understand, right now, the thought of school tomorrow is difficult for you. I am glad you told me this, because together we can work this out. I hope you have a lovely night's sleep. I will look in on you in a little while and hope to see you fast asleep." A smile, a hug, a pat on the head or whatever physical contact your child likes should be given, and leave the room.

If the child is willing to engage in further exploration then proceed in a problem-solving manner:

> Mother: "Ayesha, sometimes children or adults can experience anxiety, which is a set of unpleasant feelings. Could this be what is happening for you?"
>
> Ayesha: "I think it might be. I was afraid to go to Fatima's for the sleepover because I might have wanted to come home again."
>
> Mother: "...and school? What are you afraid of in school?"
>
> Ayesha: "I get a funny feeling in my tummy and I want to go to the toilet and we can only go to the toilet once or at break time and I feel I want to go when I get the funny feeling and..." (crying now)
>
> Mother: "You poor thing. But you are so brave for telling me this. We can make this better and you will have learned such a wonderful skill for life. There will always be times in our lives when we feel afraid or uncomfortable and we don't know how to manage it. What did you do in school today when you got this feeling?"
>
> Ayesha: "It was horrible and I felt like crying, but everyone would have laughed at me. I had to wait until

the bell went to go to the bathroom. But I am afraid that tomorrow I won't be able to do that and then I will start to cry and everyone will laugh."

Mother: "Be very proud of yourself for managing today, Ayesha. That was a big deal and you managed it. I think you are amazing to have done that all by yourself."

Ayesha: "But what if it happens again tomorrow...?"

Mother: "You will remind yourself of how you managed today. Can you think of anything else that might help you?"

Ayesha: "I don't know... And if I can't manage it... the class will know... and..." (tears again)

Mother: "I am so sorry that you have to go through this, Ayesha. I know it can be terrifying. That is the thing with anxiety, it is the thought of what might happen that makes it so terrifying."

Ayesha: "Yeah..."

Mother: "Would it help if teacher knew and she could support you in getting through the day?"

Ayesha: "Would she laugh at me?"

Mother: "I think it is very important that we explain this to her. You never know, she might know more about anxiety than we think. A lot of people have suffered/are suffering from it. Anyway, I am very sure she will be happy to help. The important thing is that you have been able to talk about this. This condition is very treatable. Sometimes it is good to go to a person like a doctor who can help us manage it, but sometimes with the help of our parents and others we can manage it ourselves."

Ayesha: "Thanks, Mammy."

Mother: "I will go to school with you in the morning and you and I can have a word with your teacher before class. Tomorrow evening we will have a good chat about a plan to help you manage this. Good night now, Ayesha. I love you very much."

Important points to note regarding how Ayesha's mother responded to her daughter's distress:

- She listened to everything Ayesha said;
- She did not minimise her daughter's fears and feelings;
- She did not try to fix the problem, instead she worked with Ayesha towards finding ways to manage it;
- She used lots of empathy;
- She educated her daughter about anxiety;
- She normalised feelings without normalising excessive worry;
- She praised her daughter for confiding in her and al-

ready working on ways to manage the problem;
- She allowed Ayesha to express her feelings and she offered appropriate comfort.

Key points

- Everyone experiences anxiety. It is a necessary and important component of being human;

- Anxiety becomes a problem when it interferes with functioning. In a child, this may include school refusal, not accepting invitations from friends to play dates or parties, excessive worry about life events and pleading with parents not to go out at night;

- Always remember, you are the most important person in your child's life. Your child may need the intervention of a therapist to help her overcome and manage distressing anxiety but she will also need you to understand anxiety and to engage with her in a problem-solving way as outlined above;

- With your support, and sometimes the intervention of an appropriate professional, your child will learn to manage his anxiety and to turn what can be very distressing to something very useful.

References

1. Hayes N. *Understand Psychology, Teach Yourself.* 5th ed. London: John Murray Learning; 2017.

2. Lester S, Russell W. *Children's Right to Play: An Examination of the Importance of Play in the Lives of Children Worldwide.* Working Papers in Early Childhood Development, No. 57. Bernard van Leer Foundation. PO Box 82334, 2508 EH, The Hague, The Netherlands; 2010 Dec.

3. Webster-Stratton C, Mostyn D, Marie JS. *The Incredible Years: A trouble-shooting guide for parents of children aged 2-8 years.* Seattle, WA: Incredible Years; 2005.

4. Carter R. *Mapping the mind.* Great Britain: Weidenfeld & Nicolson; 1998 (p21).

5. Barac R, Bialystok E. Bilingual effects on cognitive and linguistic development: Role of language, cultural background, and education. *Child development* 2012; 83(2): 413-22.

6. Government of Ireland. *Education (Welfare Act), 2000.* Dublin: The Stationery Office, 2000.

7. Biddulph, S. *Raising Boys in the 21st Century.* New York: HarperCollins Publishers; 2018.

8. Oxford English Dictionary [https://en.oxforddictionaries.com/definition/attention]

9. EarlyBird parenting programme [https://www.autism.org.uk/earlybird]

10. Valli K, Revonsuo A, Pälkäs O et al. The threat simulation theory of the evolutionary function of dreaming: Evidence from dreams of traumatized children. *Conscious Cogn* 2005; 14(1): 188-218.

11. Hartmann E. Nightmare after trauma as paradigm for all dreams: a new approach to the nature and functions of dreaming. *Psychiatry* 1998; 61(3): 223-38.

12. Citizens Information: Bullying in schools [http://www.citizensinformation.ie/en/education/primary_and_post_primary_education/attendance_and_discipline_in_schools/bullying_in_schools_in_ireland.html]

13. *Diagnostic And Statistical Manual of Mental Disorders: DSM-5*. Arlington, VA: American Psychiatric Publishing, 2013.

14. O'Brien C. Ireland's teenage anxiety problem. *The Irish-Times*. May 26, 2018.

15. Nolan M. The age of anxiety. *The Sunday Times Magazine*. Jun 3, 2018.

16. Le Doux J. *The Emotional Brain*. Great Britain: Weidenfeld & Nicolson; 1998.

Recommended reading, parenting programmes & websites

General parenting books

- Webster-Stratton C. *The Incredible Years: A Trouble Shooting Guide for Parents of Children aged 3-8 Years.* USA: The Incredible Years; 2005.

- Sharry J. *Positive Parenting: Bringing Up Responsible, Well-Behaved & Happy Children.* Ireland: Veritas; 2008.

- Lewis D. *The Secret Language of Your Child: How Children Talk Before They Can Speak.* London: Souvenir Press; 2015.

- Liedloff J. *The Continuum Concept.* London: Penguin UK; 2004

- Faber A, Mazlish E. *How to Talk So Kids Will Listen and Listen So Kids Will Talk.* London: Templar Publishing; 2012.

- Faber A, Mazlish E. *Siblings Without Rivalry: How to Help Your Children Live Together So You Can Live Too.* London: Piccadily Press; 1999.

- Biddulph, S. *Raising Boys in the 21st Century*. New York: HarperCollins Publishers; 2018.

- Biddulph, S. *Raising Girls*. New York: HarperCollins Publishers; 2013.

Books for parents and anxious children

- Huebner, D. *What to Do When You Worry Too Much: A Kid's Guide to Overcoming Anxiety*. Washington: American Psychological Association; 2005.

This is an interactive self-help book designed to guide six-to-12-year-olds and their parents through the cognitive-behavioural techniques most often used in the treatment of generalised anxiety. Engaging, encouraging, and easy to follow, this book educates, motivates, and empowers children to work towards change. It includes a note to parents by psychologist and author, Dawn Huebner, PhD.

General parenting programmes & websites

- www.incredibleyears.com

The Incredible Years parenting programme is an excellent evidence-based group parenting programme which I highly recommend. It was developed in Seattle, US, by Dr. Carolyn Webster-Stratton and has been applied in more than 20 countries, including Ireland. Its website is also excellent, where you can access some very useful handouts.

- www.circleofsecurityinternational.com

Circle of Security has an excellent parenting programme which is centred on building a secure relationship with your child from birth. The website contains some short videos which you may find helpful.

- www.rollercoaster.ie

An Irish-based online parenting resource with a lot of useful information from pre-conception onwards.

- www.parentplus.ie

Parent Plus is an evidence-based Irish parenting programme. For more information, please visit the website.

Recommended for parents of children with autism spectrum disorder

Reading

- Stillman W. *Demystifying the Autistic Experience*. London: Jessica Kingsley Publishers; 2003.
- Grandan T. *Thinking in Pictures*. London: Bloomsbury

Publishing; 2009.

- Hoopmann K. *All Cats have ASD*. London: Jessica Kingsley Publishers; 2006.

- Jackson L. *Freaks, Geeks and Asperger Syndrome: A User Guide to Adolescence*. London: Jessica Kingsley Publishers; 2002.

- Higaskida, N. *The Reason I Jump: One boy's voice from the silence of autism*. London: Sceptre; 2014.

- Hadden M. *The Curious Incident of the Dog in the Night-time*. London: Vintage Random House; 2003. (The author says that this book is about difference and seeing the world in a different way, and not about any specific disorder. However, it is a very interesting and enlightening read.)

Parenting programmes

- EarlyBird

The EarlyBird parenting programme is an excellent programme for the parents of children aged up to 6 who have a diagnosis of autism spectrum disorder (ASD). This programme is delivered in a group setting, once a week at 2.5-hour sessions for a maximum of eight weeks by trained facilitators. It aims to educate parents on ASD and to give parents a toolbox of strategies for helping their child cope in a world that presents challenges to the child on the spectrum. For more information please visit https://www.autism.org.uk/earlybird. The EarlyBird Plus is for parents of children who got the ASD diagnosis after school age and is suitable for parents of a child aged up to 10 years.

Please check with the service your child attends if it is running the EarlyBird programme.

Organisations and websites

- AsIam.ie

This very active and excellent organisation can be accessed at www.asiam.ie. The aim of AsIam is to provide a one-stop shop for the autism community in Ireland. Its website is well worth a visit, and becoming an active member of the organisation will pay dividends for parents and for people with a diagnosis of ASD.

- Aspire

Aspire has been supporting people with a diagnosis of Asperger syndrome and their families since 1995. Its website www.aspireireland.ie has some excellent information.

- Middletown Centre for Autism

This is a north-south educational initiative which was established in 2007. For further details on the work of the centre and some excellent online material visit the website at www.middletownautism.com.

Printed in Great Britain
by Amazon

51634435R00130